TILEHURST

A History

S U E   H A N D S C O M B

First published in the United Kingdom in 1995
Alan Sutton Publishing Limited
This edition published by the author.

Sue Handscomb, 2 New Lane Hill, Tilehurst, Reading, Berkshire RG30 4JF

ISBN 0 9533957 1 5

Other titles by the same author

This Was Tilehurst

Produced by MRM Associates Ltd., Unit C4, Weldale Street, Reading, Berkshire RG1 7BX

Contents

Acknowledgements

This book would not have come into being had it not been for an enquiry by Mrs Eunice Wark. My thanks go to her, to the patient and knowledgeable staff of the Royal County of Berkshire Cultural Services, Library and Information Service and the Royal County of Berkshire Record Office, and to the many residents of Tilehurst who have so generously given their time to recall memories.

As for the pictures, my thanks again go to the residents of Tilehurst who have entrusted me with their personal photographs, also to The Museum of Rural Life at Reading University, Reading Museum, Mr Kenneth Major for his photographs of Tilehurst potteries and Mr Graham Parlour for the loan of his marvellous collection of postcards.

Last but not least I thank Miss Pat Andrews, Mr Geoff Havers and Mr David Ridgus for taking the time to read the draft so purposefully. Any errors I claim as my own.

Sue Handscomb

Introduction

Humans were in or passing through the area west of Reading and now known as Tilehurst in the prehistoric age. They left as evidence a flint axe found in the Norcot Road area, a hand axe in what is now Oak Tree Road and flint tools in the area of Cockney Hill, as well as a bronze age spear found in the River Thames. There is also tangible evidence of a Roman presence in the district – remains of Roman pottery have been found at The City, a coin dating from the time of Emperor Hadrian was unearthed in St Michael's Cemetery and other Roman remains were found at Pincents Farm, Honey End Lane and Prospect Park. These people were possibly travelling between London and Silchester, and it is thought that the name The City may have derived from a Roman settlement there at the time. A Saxon sword was found at Tilehurst station.

The Domesday Book of 1085 makes no mention of Tilehurst, but it could have been included as one of the settlements in the manor of Reading. By 1291 it is included by name in its own right as a hamlet. In the thirteenth century there is a

An unrecognizable 'Reading Road' in Tilehurst.

record of a place called Tygelhurt; this changed to Tyghelhurst in the fourteenth century and to Tylehurst in the sixteenth century. In Old English 'tygel' meant tile and 'hurst' a wooded hill, so it was either 'a place in the woods where tiles were made' or 'a wooded hill where tiles were made'. Although the type of clay found in the area makes it feasible to believe that tiles were made here at that early stage, it is only the name that suggests this was happening at that time – there is no other evidence to hand. The wooded hill is easily imagined as one drives along the M4 today between junctions 11 and 12.

Reading Abbey had been founded in 1121, and was to become one of the wealthiest and most important monasteries in medieval England. The Benedictine monks were well known for their generous hospitality. The Abbots had acquired their wealth thanks to efficient administration of various land and property that they owned in Berkshire, Kent, Warwickshire and, at one time, Scotland. They also exercised exclusive rights in the cutting of furze on Tilehurst Heath. One can imagine journeying from the town of Reading, climbing the hill up to the heathlands. The layers of 'London beds' (as the sub-soil is termed) were like plasticine, the water springing up where it could. Only a few dwellings were dotted around, with most people earning their living from the land.

In 1643 during the Civil War the town of Reading was besieged. How involved Tilehurst was in these activities is uncertain, although as there was fighting in

Part of the original village at the beginning of the century.

Reading and in Theale it seems probable that there were other troop movements along the Bath Road. Residents in this area must have been drawn in to some extent, and it is quite possible that Southcote Manor, fortified by a moat, was involved.

It seems reasonable to assume too that William of Orange, with his Dutch and British troops, passed through Tilehurst in 1688 on his way from Devon to London during his bloodless revolution to claim the throne of England.

The boundaries of Tilehurst have changed over the years, and there is considerable blurring of ecclesiastical and civic confines. Broadly speaking, the east to west boundary is taken to run from Prospect Park to Theale, with the north to south borders running from the Thames to the Kennet. The Thames is really the only natural boundary, Tilehurst having grown bit by bit to fill nearly the whole area.

In the early part of this century, there were four main areas of Tilehurst: the original area surrounding St Michael's Church, The City, The Village (the area around Armour Road, Norcot Road, Recreation Road and School Road) and 'Tilehurst on Thames'. The first and last of these were considered the more 'exclusive' areas, but in reality everyone knew everyone else, although children from the different areas were wary of meeting one another. Those from The City were regarded with particular suspicion as the district had an even rougher reputation than Tilehurst itself at the time.

After the First World War many housing developments were started, a trend which increased after the Second World War and contributed to the large area Tilehurst now occupies. Although it may be viewed as another suburban sprawl, many residents still refer to it as The Village.

Two small areas of conservation can be found, one in the Routh Lane area, the other at the bottom end of New Lane Hill, but the observant will be able to find many tucked away cottages and groups of houses, decorative brickwork and distinctive tiles, footpaths and small copses – all reminders of an age that is past.

A map of 1883.

CHAPTER ONE

Open Spaces

Originally most of the land around Tilehurst was rough and uncultivated with many springs, ponds and wells which enabled the furze to grow in abundance. As time went on and some of the furze was cleared it became possible to cultivate the earth.

Maps dating from the mid-1700s show St Michael's Church with the very small development surrounding it marked as 'Tilehurst'. Beyond this, Langley Hill is marked, as are Tilehurst Common, Little Heath, Kentwood Common and Kentwood Grove, Northcot, Grove Land, Pegs Green, Honey End, Cockney Hill and Worlds End. Each was probably viewed as a separate hamlet.

By the end of the 1800s Tilehurst was still centred around the church, this area marked as Churchend. Calcot Park and Prospect Park were both established, and the area known as Harmour was just a small development alongside the pottery works. A few farms appeared – Halls, Hallplace, Kentwood, Norcot, Fords, Churchend, Fox and Honeyend. Most of these names still remain with the exception of Fords Farm, which was situated along Churchend Lane and is sometimes confused with another Fords Farm after which the present-day estate south of the Bath Road was named.

Apart from these cultivated parts there was a large area known as Tilehurst Common which extended from Westwood Road to Armour Hill. In about 1824 a

An afternoon out in Blundells Wood.

particularly noisy religious sect from a Reading chapel met on Tilehurst Common to wait for the end of the world as they had predicted. Nothing happened.

There were also many copses and woods including Blundells Copse, where there was a small gravel pit which today has been replaced by an attractive stream crossed by a wooden bridge, Lousehill Copse and Round Copse. Although these and others still exist they are somewhat reduced in size. Copses which no longer exist include Hildens, Great Birch, Garstons, Alder, Withy, Olivers, Kiln, Workhouse, Churchend and Stoneham, although again many of these names live on in different forms.

Much of the remaining land was rough scrub, and there were two pits known as Juniper and Maybough Pits.

WELLS AND PONDS

Mains water arrived in Tilehurst in 1894. Prior to this, water had been supplied from the numerous ponds and wells in the area, which many residents recall. For some years the wells were the only source of good clean water, which had to be drawn up by bucket. In 1897 a man was found drowned in Roakes Well. The well had to be cleaned out and chalk put down it to purify the water. Some of the wells are still in existence today.

Some of the ponds are also remembered, particularly one known as Broad Pool, situated at the back of The Bear Inn. It was used by the children for tadpoling and skating, but was considered dangerous and eventually filled in, probably in the early 1900s. The horse trough which replaced it can still be seen.

The Sheep Wash, which was the parish pond found in Lower Armour Road, needed cleaning out frequently. It too was replaced by a horse trough. The pond at the bottom of Bramble Crescent was known as the Withies, and had kingcups and flags.

There are many instances of water causing problems to roads. The houses built in Halls Road were set back because of the springs rising up. Chapel Hill used to flood down to The Gutter, where children used an old tool-box to float across the water. Victoria Road was often under water. There was a pond at the top of Pierces Hill, where the water frequently poured across the road. Even the cemetery did not escape – it was reported in 1911 that 'there is water in graves dug in Tilehurst'. It was a very wet area.

AGRICULTURAL GROWTH

From the early to mid–1900s Tilehurst became increasingly an area of farms and smallholdings. Many of these are recalled by the older residents of Tilehurst.

Probably the biggest farm in the area was Norcot, Minchin's or Mitchell's Farm. Its land extended from near the lower end of Norcot Hill (across where the golf links were behind Pulsometers Works) and across the road, which was then just a winding lane, taking in Broomfield Road and part of Thirlmere Avenue up to Gipsy Lane. The cow shed was on one side of the lane and the farmhouse on the other. It was ideal for the children to go tobogganing in the buttercup field here in the winter. For many years the first bus stop on Norcot Hill was referred to as 'The Farm', although the property itself had long gone.

A family picnic in the field belonging to the Rouths behind the Rectory, 1910.

Rouths Farm was behind St Michael's Church and included land where The Meadway now runs. On the corner of what is now Routh Lane was a dairy where you could buy milk at ½d per pint can or 1d for a quart can. Turnhams, or Cambridge Farm had cattle and also sold milk.

Seemingly out of Tilehurst at that time, Park Farm was situated opposite where the water tower stands today. This farm also kept cattle. It was surrounded by a high hedge, with Halls Road alongside being a small track leading to just one house. Beyond the farm lay gorse and pine woods. There were pigs and fruit trees along City Road, and cattle and pigs at Firlands at the top of Langley Hill.

Sheep were kept on Westwood or Maskell's Farm. The farmhouse stood where Hartslock Way is now built, the farm itself continuing further down the hill to Oak Tree Road. Part of Overdown Road runs across an area originally owned by Menzies Farm, then used for growing corn.

Fox Farm, also known as Cooper's Farm, was at the top of Cockney Hill where Usk Road now runs. The farm's water supply came from a well in the front garden, and people recall buying quantities of cabbages for 6d.

Hall Place Farm was recalled by evacuees who used to go and stook corn and generally help out in the summer months. This farm is not to be confused with Halls Farm, which stood where Fairway Avenue is today.

Fords Farm, also known as Smewings Farm, stood at the end of Church End Lane and covered the area now occupied by the Church of the Latter Day Saints and the tennis courts. The farm had a large duck pond, kept turkeys and grew fruit.

Kentwood Farm was not really a farm by this time, but chickens were still kept there. It was part way down Kentwood Hill, and the farmhouse is still standing today, opposite an old chalk pit. At the end of Long Lane towards Purley was Menpes Fruit Farm.

Kentwood, built in 1723 and still standing, is a Domesday site.

A footpath through The Moors.

The pool in Prospect Park, 1917. (D/L 172. The Rural History Centre, University of Reading)

There were pig or poultry farms on what was The Moors (around the present Moorlands school), where Beverley Road now stands, at Brooksby Road and where Chepstow Road is today. Also there were cornfields between Burghfield Road and Circuit Lane opposite Prospect Park.

As well as farms there were also many nurseries, smallholdings and orchards. The most notable of these was Timmers, a tree nursery, which was situated at the junction of Church End Lane with Norcot Road and used a lot of the land that is now Chichester Road. Timmers had fruit, rose and ornamental trees.

Many families had a large enough plot of land to enable them to keep their own pigs or ducks and certainly to grow vegetables. Many also kept horses in small paddocks, one of which was at the end of St Michael's Road where the crescent is now.

PARKS AND RECREATION GROUNDS

Prospect Park

When Frances Kendrick died in the mid-1700s her husband, Benjamin Child, inherited the Kendrick family estate, which consisted partly of a farm with a house known as Diles. A map of 1790 shows a small area known as Prospect Hill, and it is here that the house which was later to form the basis of the Mansion House, was first built in the 1750s. The land was bought by John Liebenrood around 1800, who built the Mansion House at about that time. However, the surrounding park was not established until 1877. Although the Mansion House gradually fell into disrepair over the years, the shell remained and it was recently entirely refurbished to make the restaurant that is there today.

The park stayed in the Liebenrood family until Major Englebert Liebenrood sold it to a speculator, Thomas Fidler, who in turn sold it to Reading Corporation in 1902 to be used as a public park. As such, part of it was let out to graze sheep, and at one time cattle as well, and this practice continued until at least 1918. During the First World War cereals were also grown in the Pegs Green area of the park. However, the park was used for a great many other purposes too: gymkhanas were held in aid of Reading Football Club, there were Temperance Festivals, the Berks, Bucks and Oxon Cross Country Association Annual Championship Race took place in the park, and the prize bands of the Temperance and Borough played there on Sunday and Wednesday evenings.

A paddling pool was introduced in 1917, which proved popular with the children. In 1919 a sapling oak which had been raised from a seed brought from Verdun was planted in the park. Bandstands were specially brought in from Palmer Park and Coley for the children's festival on Coronation Day in 1937. Today the park continues to be used for all kinds of leisure activities.

On the Bath Road border of the park is a milestone which dates back to the middle of the last century and gives the information to travellers: 'Reading 2, Newbury 15 and London 41'.

Calcot Park

This land, known as a very fine park with deer from before 1790, was also inherited by Benjamin Child as part of the Kendrick estate. The original Mansion House was built by Sir Peter Vanlore about 1620. When Sir John Blagrave purchased the estate, along with the manor of Tilehurst, in 1759 he pulled down the old house and built the present Mansion House. It remained in the Blagrave family until 1919. When the

The Mansion House as a private residence, Calcot Park.

The Hospital Sunday Parade at Victoria Recreation Ground, 1930.

estate was then put up for sale, it consisted of some 323 acres of land stocked with over 100 deer, the Mansion House and other buildings. Surprisingly at this time, it was sold to a German who later sold it to a consortium who turned it into an 18-hole golf-course in 1929. The Mansion House was used as the clubhouse until a purpose-built one was created in 1960, at which time the house was converted into flats.

Victoria Recreation Ground

This area was originally open land for grazing before being taken over by the Poors Land Charity. In 1896–7 the Trustees of the charity asked the then tenant if he would agree to give up his lease so that it could be made into a recreation ground as part of the celebrations for Queen Victoria's diamond jubilee. The Trustees paid a fee of £4 and the recreation ground was made. The ground was taken over by the Council in 1914, with part of it being converted for use as allotments in 1919, which still remain today.

This ground has been well used over the years, not just as a recreation ground for sporting activities, but also for fêtes and festivals, notably the Hospital Parades which took place each year until the creation of the National Health Service in 1948, when a husband and wife would pay 2d, and a family 3d per week. To help cover their

A view from Norcot water tower to Victoria Recreation Ground, *c.* 1910.

costs, the hospitals organized weekly parades when they would collect contributions from the crowd. Collectors used to compete with one another to see who could collect the most. The parade would go round Armour Road, Westwood Road, School Road, Recreation Road and Norcot Road, finishing in the recreation ground. Bags would be held up on poles to collect from those watching from upstairs windows.

CHAPTER TWO

Roads

EARLY ROUTES

One of the oldest roads known in the Tilehurst area is the Ancient Reading Way. Described as 'a track probably as old as the hills', this thoroughfare came down from the Ridgeway through Hermitage, Bucklebury Common and Theale, climbing up to Tilehurst along what is now Pincents Lane. Descending Pegs Green Lane, which itself wound round the area where Prospect Park was later established via the route that part of Honey End Lane now takes, the Ancient Reading Way finally ran into what is now Tilehurst Road.

Roads in the 1800s were few and far between. Tilehurst could be approached up any one of eight hills: Cockney, New Lane, Langley, Pincents, Sulham, Purley, Kentwood or Norcot; not all are named on the maps. In Tilehurst the only named roads were Dark Lane, Park Lane, Chapel Hill, Gipsy Lane, Church End Lane, Pegs Green Lane and Grovelands Lane, with many small lanes and footpaths between. Prior to the development of the road system, one simply had to walk or ride across the fields and scrubland, often using inns as landmarks, negotiating ditches and other obstacles on the way. The routes taken by many of these tracks and pathways have altered gradually over the years and the hills themselves have become flatter.

During the reign of George III turnpikes allowed private individuals to maintain

A very rural Kentwood Hill with only the farmhouse in sight.

Gipsy Lane, part of which remains almost unchanged today.

parts of a road and charge a toll for the privilege of using it. One of the most important roads in the Tilehurst area at the time was the London to Bath road, a small section of which ran from Reading to Theale. The road became more significant as Bath became fashionable as a spa town in the Georgian period. Although this road did improve, like all roads it remained very dusty and pumps were installed at regular intervals, providing water to keep down the dust. Several were to be seen along the Bath Road, one near the corner of Burghfield Road, and two opposite Prospect Park. One still remains by the roadside at Calcot. From 1815 road surfaces were further improved by John McAdam's method of re-surfacing.

Bath Road at The Horncastle, *c.* 1910.

PROBLEMS WITH THE ROADS

New properties were being built increasingly of brick. The demand for the wares of the Tilehurst potteries was high and in the late 1800s, as the industry became increasingly active to cope with demand, the surrounding roads began to take a hammering. Goods were transported from the factories mostly by road-rail, using traction engines. As these were heavy machines which ran on iron wheels they caused considerable damage to the road surface. The state of the road running to Pangbourne caused much consternation.

From 1892 onwards there were numerous complaints about the state of some roads and demands that more money be spent on repairs. Concerns were expressed initially about the Reading to Wallingford road, that it should be upgraded to a main road, and then about the excessively heavy traffic that the road between Tilehurst and Pangbourne was taking. In 1897 a Berkshire Council report stated:

> The road has been greatly damaged by extraordinary traffic . . . was authorised to provide such extra material and labour . . . The traction engine traffic continues to cut up the road and Mr Tollit is taking note of the damage done by the several engines.

A little later a second report read:

> . . . Heaviest and most trying traffic . . . owing to the numerous building operations at and about Pangbourne, this road is almost daily traversed by Traction Engines drawing bricks and great injury is done by them to the road . . . I am also having particulars taken as to the Engines using this road in view of proceedings being taken, and I have given notice to the Owners.

In 1899 it was suggested by Berkshire Council that a conference be called to discuss:

> traction engine traffic and the damage thereby occasioned to the roads owing to the unjust (to the ratepayers) conditions under which it is worked, with a view to sending a deputation to the local Government Board.

It was not thought advisable to do this at that time, however, and the problems with the traction engine traffic continued.

In 1901 an action was instigated against Messrs Brewerton, Wickens and Cox with regard to damage from extraordinary traffic. This had to be withdrawn, however, because of technical difficulties in connection with the evidence. A report in 1904 states that 'The Wallingford Road is in fair shape but much disturbed by continuous traction engine traffic which the limestone used cannot possibly stand.' In 1906 'One of the three small bridges known as Chain Arches that nearest Reading broke after an engine belonging to the Tilehurst Haulage Company had passed over it.' The repair estimate was £10 to £12.

By 1912 Berkshire County Council were obviously getting exasperated by the constant demand on their money made by just one road:

> With reference to heavy traction engine traffic by engines not licensed in the County and paying the statutory fee of 2/6d a day . . . in any case, the payment . . . is wholly inadequate

Oxford Road before it was widened in 1917.

to meet the damage done to the roads by this traffic and under certain weather conditions the result has been found to be deplorable . . . remedial legislation may be introduced.

In 1912 two drivers of traction engines were fined £1 each for speeding in the Tilehurst Road. It would be interesting to know at what speed they were travelling.

In 1916 a claim was made against the county council after an incident outside the Plough Inn:

> We beg to notify you of damage to a wheel of one of our pantec. vans caused through your waterman allowing the water from a watercart to fall over our horses' legs thereby frightening them and causing them to swerve, dragging the van into the wall of the house.

THROWING LIGHT ON THE SUBJECT?

Gas street lighting had been suggested in Tilehurst as early as 1900, but the notion was turned down by the parish council. However, it reversed its decision in 1903, adding 3*d* to the rates for all ratepayers to cover the expenses of the first year. The lamps were to operate for nine months and then be stored and refitted when required. Once the lamps were in use residents started wanting more, which eventually they got, despite the fact that certain members of the community used them for target practice. Unfortunately, these activities only added to the cost of maintenance, which was already higher than in nearby Reading because the lamps 'are so few and far apart so a lamplighter can only light 44 lamps as compared with 95 lamps in Reading'. By 1904 some oil lamps had been added and by the end of 1906 lamps were distributed as follows:

> Norcot Lane 16, Recreation Road 3, Kentwood Hill 3, School Road 8, Chapel Hill 1, Church Road 8, Westwood Road 3, Victoria Road 2, Armour Road 3, Lower Armour 2 with 1 extra added in Crescent Road.

Church Road in the 1920s. This is now St Michael's Road.

The straight Westwood Road, *c.* 1910.

A recognizable Norcot Road from the 1900s.

CHANGES OF DIRECTION

As well as the fluctuating condition of the roads, over the years residents of Tilehurst have had to contend with the development of the road system as a whole as well as changes to existing roads.

Some roads have been renamed completely: Straight Street is now Westwood Road, Deadmans Lane now Dark Lane, Tuppenny Pightle now Oak Tree Road, School End now Downing Road, Norcot Lane and Hilltop now Norcot Road. Tilehurst Road was first known as Pigs Green Lane, then Pegs Green Lane, before taking on its present-day name. Although many new roads have been built, especially as part of the new estates that have been developed, many of the current street names still recall old farms, houses or particular features of the area.

Church Road, which no longer exists, used to wind round from the point of The Triangle along where it has now been pedestrianized to join St Michael's Road, and then all the way down to the church and to the top of New Lane Hill, which at that time started at the top of Cockney Hill. On the 1900 map Church Road was called Back Road, but this seems to have been an error.

St Michael's Road was a very short road and was extended to take in part of Church Road, while Church End Lane no longer goes all the way to the church since The Meadway cut across it.

Church Road. In 1911 this road wound its way from The Triangle to St Michael's Church. It is now the top of New Lane Hill.

Church End Lane beside some of the Rectory outbuildings in the 1930s.

In recent years the building of The Meadway, Mayfair and Overdown Road as major roadways has increased accessibility for road users. The development of The Meadway in the 1960s, for example, opened up a new way from Reading to Tilehurst. Some residents were amazed at the choice of route as it would surely involve a very steep drop near the end of Church End Lane. When the road was constructed, however, the incline just disappeared – the engineers simply smoothed it out.

Honey End Lane used to wind its way from the Bath Road going round by Prospect Park Hospital, until the Meadway Shopping Centre was built and the lane was cut in two. Another section of the road was taken straight through.

The junction of School Road with Westwood Road, *c.* 1930.

FOOTPATHS AND LANES

As well as the roads, numerous lanes and footpaths were used in the area. From the end of Downing Road a footpath led over a wooden bridge which crossed a stream (The Gutter) and then up by the Royal Oak. Another well-used path ran from the back of Routh Farm near the corner of what is now Routh Lane, coming down the big slope there and then out at the bottom of Water Road. It was then possible to walk up Grovelands and down to catch the tram at the Pond House. At one point the path branched, the other section coming out onto the Tilehurst Road opposite Prospect Park.

In 1972 there was some dispute over Lovers Lane, which ran from Routh Lane through to Grovelands. Mrs Freda Routh, whose late husband's grandfather had been Rector, claimed that, if Lovers Lane and another road had not been privately built by her husband's family, St Michael's Estate could never have been built, and she claimed a very large sum, by way of compensation. The case might have progressed almost unnoticed had it not been for the way in which it was conducted. It is reported that Mrs Routh:

> appeared at the hearing carrying a wooden spear. She said she was carrying it for protection against her fight against officialdom. She had also astounded the tribunal by cross-examining herself. She asked herself questions in a loud strident voice – and then answered herself in a softer feminine tone.

Mrs Routh was finally awarded a very small amount as compensation.

CHAPTER THREE

Transport

WATER

Until the eighteenth century few controls were enforced along the River Thames. In 1751, however, a special body of Thames commissioners was set up comprising officials from the main towns along the river from Staines upstream. Various Acts were gradually introduced to aid navigation. Old flash weirs were purchased from their owners and new locks added. The first steam boats were seen in 1813. 'Tilehurst on Thames' appears to have been a very attractive area, with a ferry across the river at The Roebuck Inn, now Beethoven's Hotel, from at least 1882. We are told in Kelly's Directory that 'The Roebuck is a new and excellent hotel for the accommodation of anglers on the banks of the Thames', and four years later that the same hotel provided 'accommodation for boating parties and families visiting this delightful neighbourhood'. Pleasure boats could be picked up at Scours Lane, and this along with other outdoor activities such as fishing, picnicking and walking made the northern boundary of Tilehurst most appealing to the residents of the time.

In the early 1700s proposals were put forward to link London with Bristol via the Avon and Thames rivers. As Bristol was fast developing into the premier port for transatlantic shipping the need to connect the two cities was becoming ever more

The ferry at The Roebuck, *c.* 1912.

necessary. At the time these proposals were suggested the River Kennet was only navigable as far as Reading, although it did flow on through the southern extreme of Tilehurst. In 1715 the Kennet Navigation Act was passed and work began on making the Kennet navigable as far as Newbury, the route finally being opened for barges in 1724. The move did not please everybody, however; the owners of mills along the river, such as the one at Calcot, were aggrieved because they had to compete with the barge owners for the limited supply of water. Initially, the waterway was also fiercely opposed by the townspeople of Reading, although eventually it helped the town to prosper, not least its brewing industry.

In the 1740s barges of up to 200 tons carried goods along the Kennet at the rate of approximately 500 barges a year. In 1794 plans for the Kennet and Avon canal were approved by Parliament and by 1810 the link between London and Bristol was completed, so adding substantially to the trade of the Kennet navigation. Although an improvement on transporting goods by road, using the canals was slow and operations were often hampered by ice, floods and storms or in dry weather by the low level of water.

But then came the railway, which caused the very quick demise of the barge. The canal had become impassable by 1940 but was reopened for leisure use in 1992. The canal and river, along with the Holy Brook, a tributary of the Kennet which also runs to the south of Tilehurst, are now used almost exclusively for boating and fishing.

RAIL

In 1824 some Bristol merchants proposed a railway to be worked by locomotives between London and Bristol. The railway could run on either side of the Thames, and whichever route was selected it would be shorter than any available road. This application, however, never materialized. A few years later, in 1832, and after several more unsuccessful suggestions, four influential businessmen – the founders of the Great Western Railway Company – met to discuss the problem, appointing Isambard Kingdom Brunel as engineer in 1833.

Brunel travelled between London and Bristol many times to determine the best possible route. A bill to approve the line was submitted to Parliament in 1834, and would have permitted the compulsory purchase of the necessary land, anyone who had any claim to any portion of that land having to be traced first. Although the bill was approved by the House of Commons, it was rejected by the House of Lords. Additional subscribers were found and both financial and moral support was secured at meetings held in all the large towns in the area. Charles Saunders, secretary of a group of prominent merchants and businessmen in London, reported the business as 'sad, harassing work . . . in pressing perfect strangers to contribute'. However, attempts were largely successful as, apart from a few opponents, most of the affected landowners agreed to give up their land.

Royal Assent was granted in August 1835 and the Great Western Railway Company was incorporated and empowered to construct its railway.

By 1840 the railway came as far as Reading and just one year later it had reached Bristol. Nine passenger and one goods train were timetabled to pass through the area each day. The passenger trains were able to transport both horses and carriages,

Tilehurst station, which was opened in 1882.

making for a far quicker and more comfortable journey for all, but passengers intending to make use of this facility had to arrive at least 10 minutes before the set departure time. As Greenwich Mean Time was not introduced until 1884 even local times varied, and so departure time had to be calculated with care – Reading was some 4 minutes behind London!

The initial GWR used a broad gauge, derived from the days of the stagecoach, unlike most of the rest of the railway system which had adopted a narrower gauge, as used in old mines. This broad gauge gave more stability and enabled the trains to run faster, but eventually even the GWR had to conform to the majority of the system, and by 1891 the narrower gauge became standard.

In May 1851 Henry Hunter and James Fuller, two 'navvies' working on the railway line, abandoned a trolley on the line near The Roebuck. The trolley was hit by an on-coming train, whose engine was damaged. Both men were summonsed and sentenced to a month's imprisonment.

The station at Tilehurst was not opened until 1882. There were just two lines, with a station building on the Down platform containing the booking office, and a simple wooden shed on the Up platform. There was a footbridge over the tracks and a house was provided nearby for the station master. The railway then installed a penny-in-the-slot gate and footpath to allow easy access to the tow-path and river. This no longer exists, the only access today being by covered footbridge over the railway alongside Beethoven's Hotel (formerly The Roebuck).

Although publicity material was originally aimed particularly at visitors, enticing the day trippers, walkers and picnickers heading for the river to use the station, the railway had a major influence on the expansion of Tilehurst as a whole for it was now possible to travel by train from Tilehurst to Reading, Oxford, London or Bath.

There was a signal-box at Tilehurst station by 1883. The box controlled the double line, but a new box was required when the line was quadrupled in 1893. It was situated on the Reading side of the station. There was an extensive goods yard at Tilehurst in 1905 when coal and coke from the collieries were stored for the coal merchants, and for use in the potteries during the period from the 1920s to the 1960s. This area is now a car-park. There was also a thriving parcels office in the early 1900s.

The exchange sidings and yard at Scours Lane came into their own during the First World War when considerably more traffic needed interchanging.

The station became very useful for commuters travelling from Tilehurst to London, one of whom was Sir Felix Pole, the General Manager of the Great Western Railway itself.

ROAD

Although the railways became a major means by which both goods and people were transported, roads remained important. In the 1900s most people in the Tilehurst area would have travelled on foot, some may have had bicycles and a few a pony and trap. Local shops would still have delivered their goods by bicycle or cart and the road system was also vital for carriers, whose job involved delivering letters and goods and collecting passengers from the stations.

Letters were despatched from Tilehurst four times per day in 1883, and there were carriers travelling from Tilehurst to Reading daily from 1887. Tom Illsley (also spelt Ilsley) was the most well-known carrier for Tilehurst and he would bring passengers or luggage from Tilehurst or Reading railway stations by horse and cart. He later had a Ford 'Tin Lizzie'. When Tom went to Calcot he had to travel along the Bath Road and up Cockney Hill as Langley Hill was both too steep and had a very poor surface.

One of the last stage-coaches from Oxford to London at The Roebuck, 1910.

Illsley the Carrier – the only transport from Tilehurst to Reading in 1900.

He had one petrol pump in School Road, where the present garage stands, and he also used to recharge radio accumulators for 4*d*.

A carrier would also collect lists of groceries from households who had indicated their need for the service, usually by putting a sign in the window. In the Tilehurst area, a house displaying an 'A' sign required the services of Aldridge, a carrier in Bath Road. Once he had collected the list, Aldridge would hand it to the shopkeeper who would make up the order. While he was waiting, Aldridge would make other deliveries or rest his horses at one of the local inns. The goods would be collected and returned to the household. The carrier would charge something like 3*d* for his service. If a carrier had space it was sometimes possible for a passenger to get a lift with him.

The transport of passengers in the Tilehurst area began in the late 1800s when a horse-drawn covered wagon made journeys between the town and Reading. Kelly's Directory of 1899 draws attention to 'a bus service twice daily to and from Reading, and on Saturdays three times'.

In Reading single-deck trams which seated twenty-four passengers and were drawn by a single horse travelled from Cemetery Junction to The Barracks in 1879; by 1890 the trams had grown into double-deckers needing two horses to pull them. In 1901 the trams were taken over by Reading Corporation and two years later the horses were taken out of service as the routes were electrified. By now the trams were running to The Pond House public house on Oxford Road by Grovelands Road. The improved transport system must have been of considerable benefit, opening up a new way of life for the people of Tilehurst. Many residents were now able to work in Reading and recall walking to and from The Pond House to catch the tram. Later, towards the end of the First World War, the trams were also used to carry parcels, and special cars were added for wounded soldiers, who travelled free of charge.

The first bus carries its passengers in Tilehurst, 1919.

By 1915 buses travelled along Oxford Road, the route running from Maidenhead to Streatley via Tilehurst and, later that year, extending to Wallingford. The buses were run by the British Automobile Traction Company, which was regionalized some five years later as the Thames Valley Traction Company Limited.

Towards the end of the First World War the decision was taken to operate motor buses on more lightly trafficked routes to the expanding areas of Reading, Tilehurst being one. 'The Motor Omnibus Service for public conveyance of passengers' commenced on 6 December 1919, the final inauguration ceremony having taken place the previous day. This was the first Reading Corporation motor bus service, and it ran between St Andrew's Church, Caversham Heights and The Plough at Tilehurst. In 1926 another route was added from Lower Caversham to Bath Road (Horn Castle). In the same year the Corporation also started a bus service which linked The Pond House and The Roebuck.

In 1930 the tram route which had come up Castle Hill and only a short way along Bath Road, terminating a little way west of the Tilehurst Road/Coley Avenue crossroads, was discontinued as the route was now well serviced by motor buses. The final tram was taken out of service from Reading in 1939.

The bus service began to expand and by 1939 trolley buses, which had been introduced in Reading in 1936, ran as far as the Bear Inn at Tilehurst. Routes were also opened up to Southcote Road, Blagrave Hospital and Hemdean Road. Residents recall the time when the trolley bus was turned at the end of Westwood Road. A long pole was used to control the cable arm. If the operator was not careful the pole would almost go through the window of the house alongside. There are still trolley bus poles on Kentwood Hill, which are now used for street lighting. They lean outwards, which would have provided tension for the overhead cables.

Westwood Road was also the terminus for the petrol buses, which would reverse

A trolleybus passing The Triangle, *c.* 1960.

into School Road. As the bus turned, the conductor blew his whistle to indicate that the road was clear. This made the children hurry to Park Lane School, thinking it might be the school whistle and that they would be late.

By 1944 the bus service was extended to include Kentwood. The further expansion of the bus routes throughout Tilehurst made it far easier for people to get from their homes into Reading to work or shop, particularly when Tilehurst Road extended into The Meadway in the 1960s, allowing the buses to circulate around the area more easily.

It was not until 1964 that Reading buses were given route numbers, and as late as 1968 that trolley buses were finally taken out of service.

The roads were increasingly used by private individuals as well as by public transport. In April 1900 over eighty vehicles left Hyde Park Corner in the first ever 1,000 mile time trial for motor vehicles, organized by the Automobile Association. The event stopped off at Calcot Park in Tilehurst where they were greeted by Alfred Harmsworth (later Lord Northcliffe, the newspaper magnate).

CHAPTER FOUR

Employment

Of all the trades and professions established in Tilehurst over the years, the potteries had the largest influence and were by far the principal industry in the area.

THE POTTERIES

Thames Valley clay had been used for brick making as far back as 1830. Mr Waugh's brickworks is marked on a map of around 1842. But Mr Samuel Wheeler moved his works from Coley into Tilehurst in 1885, Mr Fred Wheeler making good flower pots and glazed bread pans. Mr Leonard Wheeler, grandson of Samuel Wheeler, founded the Tilehurst Potteries Limited (1922) Company, which grew very rapidly. In 1928 there were some 50 staff, and by 1936 there were over 200, mostly paid on piece work. At that time wages were good, training was given and the workers were well looked after, although discipline was said to be very strict. However, as work in the factory was potentially dangerous, this was probably no bad thing.

Despite the fact that by 1936 over 20,000,000 pieces a year were being produced, the company was hardly keeping pace with the demand for tiles, which were used to tile such places as Chequers, Radley College, the Royal Masonic School at Rickmansworth, Sydney Sussex College at Cambridge, the Middle Temple in London, the Radcliffe Infirmary at Oxford and the Fire Headquarters at Birmingham.

The firm was mostly known for its hand-made, sand-faced roofing tiles, which were made from the clay bed adjoining the works. The success of the tiles was said to be because of the texture and low porosity of the clay. A variety of shades and colours, described as red, multi-coloured, mixed and antique, were obtained by burning the tiles for different periods of time or by adding different coloured sand.

The clay was originally dug from the pit by hand, but later a Ruston-Bucyrus digger was operated at the clay face. The clay still had to be removed by shovel, however, being loaded into metal skips which were pushed on roads made from oil drums sunk into the ground and covered with railway sleepers. The skips were hooked up to a continuous running wire rope, pulled to the top of the gantry, and their contents tipped into the pug mill.

The pug mill consisted of a series of rollers and gratings, through which the clay was crushed to remove air and impurities. The rollers weighed several tons each, and once the engines had started up they caused not only heavy vibrations, but also a noise that could be heard well into the surrounding area.

The clay was forced out of a 'mouth' about a foot square, cut off by hand using a

A Tilehurst potteries clay pit, with a line of the rail track and the Priestman digger.

wire and fed through another rolling machine where it was mixed with water and a proportion of sand to make it the right consistency to be taken to the 'bat' machine. The 'bat' machine extruded the clay in a slab about 9 in wide by 1 in thick, which then ran on rollers and was cut by a wire into 4 ft lengths. Another cutter was then pulled over, cutting the 4 ft slab into eight pieces, which were called 'bats'. The 'bats' were stacked on the floor ready for collection, when they were taken on a board to the tiler's workbench.

The 'bats' were then dropped into moulds, to which fish oil had been applied to prevent the clay from sticking. Once in the mould the 'bat' was shaped with a 'batter', which also had a wire attached to remove excess clay. The tiles were then pushed out of the mould with a foot-operated lever, and placed on boards and then on to a barrow to be wheeled into the drying shed. The barrow carried about 100 tiles.

An experienced tiler could turn out 1,200 to 1,500 tiles a day, for 10s per thousand. The making of special tiles, such as ridge tiles, required particular skills and the rates of pay reflected this – 3 to 4s per hundred, according to type.

There was an outsize boiler – probably one of the biggest in the south of England at that time – capable of evaporating 10,000 lb of water per hour. Every year 6,000 tons of coal were burned to produce steam which was conveyed beneath the drying room.

The pottery stood apart from the tile-making area. Only twelve potters were employed. They used kick wheels mostly to make flower pots, some large bowls, bread pans, honey pots and chimney pots. A boy helped the potter to prepare the clay by 'wedging' it before the potter threw it – sometimes pieces as heavy as 20 to 30 lb – and also carried the clay away to dry.

Chimney pots up to 4 ft high had to be made in two sections, which were joined

A bench with some of the tools of the trade of a tilemaker.

the following day. All the pieces were left to dry on wooden battens for up to a week, and were then stacked in the kiln room for firing.

Gangs of men carried out the different types of work. The filling and emptying of the kiln was termed 'setting' and 'drawing', and the gang who did this stacked the tiles around the edge of the circular chamber. The pots required more careful handling. Much of the work was paid on piece rate, so had to be carried out on the run, each gang relying on the work of another.

After the kiln was loaded, the hatchway was sealed and the kiln was fired through several firing holes. Over a period of three days the temperature was gradually raised until 1,000 °C was reached on the third day. This was held for two days before the kiln was allowed to cool by lifting and dropping a damper fitted to the flue of each kiln and directed to the tall chimneys.

Each year thousands of the 12 inch flower pots were sent to the Channel Islands, where they were used to grow tomatoes, and also to Kew Gardens and the royal parks in London. The nurseries in Tilehurst also took regular deliveries. Damaged pots and tiles, and unused clay, were collected up, soaked and made into bricks.

Work was said to be very strenuous, dirty and boring, the potters working all day with arms covered in wet clay. There were no washing facilities, and when hot water was required it was heated in buckets on the kiln firing holes. The kiln area itself was excessively hot and dry to work in.

Working hours were Monday to Friday, 7 a.m. to 5 p.m. and Saturday, 7 a.m. to 12.30 p.m. Workers were paid 2s an hour. There was a breakfast break of half an hour and a dinner break from 12 p.m. to 1 p.m. Workers took packed food and a bottle of tea for their breaks, although sometimes they were beaten to it by the rats.

The great workshop at Tilehurst potteries, with the kilns.

A bell was rung to indicate the times and all the workers had to clock in by card. The cards were collected five minutes after the morning bell; any late workers lost half an hour's pay.

At the start of the Second World War the pottery gradually closed down as the men were called up for service.

Local people referred to the pottery as 'The Treacle Mines', possibly because of the thick yellow colour of the clay that stuck to everything. It turned out to be almost prophetic as, during the war, Tate and Lyle Ltd used the drying shed at Kentwood kiln to store sugar. A firm called Motor-Metalcraft also rented a small part of the building when it was bombed out of its premises in Willesden. This firm was joined by John Lancaster Radiators.

The pottery reopened with improved facilities after the war. However, although business initially flourished it became very difficult to obtain workers for the type of work required, and plastic pots also began to appear on the market. The pottery section was closed in 1963. The tile department remained very busy, but following a fire in 1966 it was learned that all work was to cease on the site and the firm was to close after 101 years because of shortage of labour. Sixty people were employed at that time, but another twenty to twenty-five were needed.

S.E. Collier was another major pottery works. It was established at Grovelands in 1870 and continued production until 1967, becoming famous for 'Colliers Reading Red' as the most common good quality clay used was bright, sandy red. One person who started work with Colliers in 1922 said that it was very hard work and not as well paid as the railways, where his brothers worked. The pottery workers started work at 6.30 a.m. and sometimes worked until 8 p.m.

Along with a smaller pottery works which stood opposite, Colliers took the clay from the area where Dee Road runs now, which was later made into golf links before the present estate was built. When the clay from this site was exhausted, Colliers turned to Norcot Hill. As this was some distance away the firm had to devise a way of transporting the clay from its pits to its premises. About twenty people worked at the pits at that time with a further hundred at Grovelands.

Around 1928–9 the raw clay was dug from the pits by a digger, put in wheelbarrows with iron wheels running on a 4 in wide strip of steel, and taken to buckets which were suspended on overhead cables which ran to Grovelands.

The aerial cable, which ran some 20–30 ft above the ground, is marked as running from the clay pit, across Norcot Road, alongside Compton Plantation where it takes a sharp turn across Lousehill Copse, across an old clay pit and what is now Water Road to Grovelands. Instead of talking about Church End Lane residents would say 'down by the buckets'.

After being carried to Grovelands, the clay was allowed to settle and weather as the water ran out of it. It was then sent to the factory to be processed and all the impurities removed so that the potters would not cut their hands on any sharp pieces; it turned out like butter. At Colliers the chimney-pots were made by hand on the wheel in three parts as it was not possible to reach right inside.

The clay pits were dug very deep; the one at Norcot, positioned where Upcroft School now stands, was estimated to be 80 ft deep. It has been described as 'something you might see from another part of the country'. Children used to go down there to collect frogs; it was rather like an adventure playground for them.

A son whose father worked as a pattern-maker at Colliers reports that his father shaped the wood from which the tile was formed. He recalls taking his father's dinner over to him, up Grovelands Road, over the cliff and down to the kiln.

There were several buildings at Grovelands. Two were potteries where very attractive decorative pottery known as 'Silchester Ware' was made. This was produced

'The buckets' over Norcot Road, 1930.

in a great variety of shapes, often imitating medieval, Greek or Roman styles, and was finished with a dark grey glaze. Another product was a type of pottery called 'Rustic Ware', these pieces being made to give the impression they had been fashioned from tree stumps.

Two of the other buildings were tile factories. Here the tiles were fired by coal or coke, coke giving out a higher temperature. The coal came from the collieries to Tilehurst station by the trainload, horses and carts and traction engines delivering it to Water Road.

During the Second World War Colliers was issued with a special contract to make bricks for air-raid shelters, which the men from the factory had to complete before they could be called up.

The Shakespeare Memorial Theatre was built of hand-made bricks from Colliers, specially burned a browny colour.

At its height Colliers ran sixteen kilns to bake the bricks. This included one of the large Hoffman kilns which could hold 200,000 bricks at one firing. Many of the buildings in Reading were made from these bricks, perhaps most notably the Town Hall.

The Honey End Lane pottery still stands facing The Meadway shopping precinct, although it is no longer active. It took its clay from the area where The Meadway now stands. The remains of this small pottery can still be seen, with the chimney and outbuildings still standing, but this last reminder of the pottery industry in Tilehurst is soon to be demolished.

OTHER EMPLOYMENT

Apart from the potteries, the main employment in Tilehurst around the turn of the century was on a farm. Kelly's Directory of 1847 shows that there were nine farmers in the area, although it also lists eleven beer retailers, a baker, grocer, bootmaker, miller, brick manufacturer, grocer and bricklayer, wheelwright and bricklayer, blacksmith, carpenter, nurseryman and shopkeeper.

At the post office, Thomas Illsley was the receiver. Letters arrived from Reading at 7 a.m. and were despatched to Reading at 7 p.m. Public houses included The New Inn, Worlds End, The Roebuck and The Bird in Hand.

By 1883 a Mrs Sarah Delaford is listed as running some coffee rooms and a Mrs Amy Hissey is given as a farmer and brick maker. Richard Roake is named as the huntsman to the South Berkshire foxhounds.

In 1887 Samuel and Edward Collier are named as brick and tilemakers at Grovelands Kiln, and Wheeler Bros, brick and tile pottery works at Kew Kiln and others at Whitley and Caversham. By this time Tilehurst also had its own oilman, medical botanist, station master, physician, market gardener, dairyman, tobacconist and coal merchant.

By 1895 there was a stud groom to the foxhounds and a whipper-in, a hairdresser, registrar of births, marriages and deaths, a haberdasher, childrens' day school attendance officer and a highway surveyor.

Evidence of the further expansion and development of the town is given in records dating from 1899, which show that there were builders and plumbers, house

A smallholding in Chapel Hill at the turn of the century.

The Fox and Hounds in City Road.

'Will you let me know by return lowest price for strawberries?'

decorators and sanitary engineers, hardware and paint dealers, poulterers and a land
steward.

The South Berkshire Hunt moved from their original kennels on the corner of
Bath Road and Burghfield Road (now Old Kennels Court) to the end of Long Lane
in 1910. The hounds were kept here until 1955 when they were moved out to
Mortimer. Some residents can remember the hunt going along Church Road each
Saturday. There were other kennels at the bottom of Pierces Hill.

FAMILY FIRMS

Although many shops, small industries and offices have come and gone in Tilehurst,
two family firms have stood the test of time and remain.

Horncastle Garage

Horncastle Garage was established on Bath Road on the site that it still occupies
today in 1926 when James West bought a plot of land at Horncastle Hamlet. He built
a family home for his seven children with a garage for his charabanc company. He
had a 1922 Fiat open charabanc and also made his own fourteen-seater charabanc. A
petrol pump was erected outside the house in 1927 so beginning the Horncastle
Garage and J. West and Sons, the builders.

Stan West, James's son, was then twenty-one, and managed the garage side of the
business for his father. Although the garage had to be closed during the Second
World War, it prospered and began to expand after it reopened in 1945.

Warings, the bakers of Armour Road.

The beginnings of Horncastle Garage.

Following the death of James West, Stan took over the garage, which became Horncastle Garage Ltd. The firm obtained an Austin franchise and later became an Austin main dealer. In 1976 it was invited to become a Ford main dealer. Stan's son-in-law, Peter Nash, managed this deal as well as increasing expansion of the site and, later, the rebuilding of the frontage. Stan West resigned as chairman in 1991 and his place was taken by his daughter, Penny, Peter Nash's widow.

Over a period of nearly seventy years this family business has grown from a simple home for a family of nine into a business now employing some 150 people.

Warings

Mr Waring came to Tilehurst in 1928 having been works manager of Harrisons, a bakery in Reading. He and his family lived in what was then Church Road. After renting a bakery in Weldale Street he was assisted financially by Arthur Newbery and started up his own bakery in Armour Road in 1932. At that time there were three other bakers in Tilehurst: Beasleys in Recreation Road, Wrights opposite the Prince of Wales public house and Rules in Norcot Road. Because nearly all the bakery's business was delivered direct to the customer, it was not thought necessary at that time to have premises on the main road. The whole family moved to Armour Road and Waring's two sons took over, although one soon moved away from the area. The bakery is still owned by the family today and bakes daily.

CHAPTER FIVE

Notable Public Buildings

BLAGRAVE HOSPITAL

The trustees of the Blagrave estate sold 5½ acres of land. Mr Herbert Blagrave gave a financial donation towards the Blagrave Hospital, which was opened in 1930 by Prince George, later to become the Duke of Kent. Originally the hospital, an extension to The Royal Berkshire Hospital, cared for patients convalescing from tubercular complaints. There were two main wards, each with thirty beds and a verandah. The hospital was sold in 1988 and demolished. Voler Drive and the adjoining development has been built on the site.

BOX GROVE

Box Grove was a convalescent home at Little Heath, set up for women and children who had tuberculosis. It was established in 1864 by the late Mrs Wilder of Purley Hall and was said to be 'beautifully sited on the brow of a hill, in a very healthy location'. The house had previously been inhabited by a retired army captain.

PARK HOSPITAL

Park Hospital occupies a 10 acre site on the edge of Prospect Park and was opened as an isolation hospital for forty patients suffering from scarlet fever or diphtheria.

Blagrave Hospital. 'This is our hospital. The mens ward is on the left and the nurses home is behind the wards. You can just see the roof. The centre room is for the kiddies and there is a small ward each side for private patients.'

Park Isolation Hospital, 1907.

Although completed in 1904, it was not officially opened until 1906. In 1916 additional huts were erected. It remained partly as an isolation hospital and partly as a general hospital until the 1980s when it was converted into an administrative headquarters for the district.

THE LITTLE OR NEW PLOUGH INN

Although advertised as 'The Plough', to distinguish it from the present Plough public house (which was originally known as The Plough Inn or The Old Plough), this establishment was known locally as 'The Little Plough'. It stood on The Triangle opposite the present Plough, along what was then Church Road, leading into St Michael's Road. Both The Old Plough and The New Plough (that is, The Little Plough) were in existence in 1861, but it is difficult to distinguish which was which.

It has been described as 'a funny little place'. A step led down from the entrance gateway into the bar, and there was a second bar just round the corner. There were some old sheds outside in which there were forms and tables. Families were able to sit out there with their children on their return from a family walk. People remember the inn kept a parrot adept at 'wolf-whistling'.

THE PRIORY

It has not been possible to trace the origin of The Priory, which stood where Keswick Close now stands. It is marked on maps as far back as 1870, and was inhabited in 1871 by a retired grocer, which does not help to explain the derivation of its name. It is known to have been used by curates from St Michael's Church at the beginning of the century during the incumbency of Revd Henry Cooper Smith, probably because he occupied the Rectory with his three unmarried daughters. When Revd Francis Sherwood took up the incumbency in 1934, however, there was

'The Little Plough', 1959.

The Plough Inn, *c.* 1910.

no longer a need for this as the curates lived with him at the Rectory. Later it belonged to a succession of doctors, but it was eventually demolished and the site used for building.

A natural spring in the grounds of The Priory formed a meandering lake on which boating took place. Children used to peep over the hedge to look at the lake and see how many birds they could spot, and if the geese had arrived. It is thought that it was this lake that drained into what was then Church Road, the houses that were built on The Priory side needing walkways over the ditch for access to the road.

THE RED BARN

No longer in existence today, The Red Barn originally held what was to become a very prominent position in Tilehurst on what is now The Triangle. It was inhabited in the 1800s by an agricultural labourer and his wife. When it was sold in 1887 it was described as 'a brick built and slated barn 37 feet long and 24 feet wide with a brick and tiled cart shed and two stall stabling with a yard or garden'. It had 'extensive frontages to three parish roads'.

THE WATER TOWERS

The 120 ft high water tower on Park Lane is a landmark which can be seen for many miles from the south. In 1902 a reservoir was built of brick to store water for the expanding population. However, this was not enough and in 1932 additional

The Park Lane water tower under construction.

The Norcot water tower, *c.* 1912. This is now a listed building.

reservoirs and the water tower were built of reinforced concrete. The reservoirs hold 22 million gallons of water, and the tower another 200,000 gallons.

There is an older brick tower off Norcot Road. This was built at the end of the last century, is 50 ft high and has recently been designated a listed building.

WESTWOOD HOUSE

Once owned by the Countess of Eldon, Westwood House stood where Fircroft Close now stands. It was later owned by a Mr Barnett, who seems to have been quite a character, often referred to as 'The Squire'. He had servants in the house.

There were stables at the back of the house and in the winter Mr Barnett would take the children for rides along Westwood Road in a horse-drawn sledge. Many of the older residents recall Mr Barnett making his way to church by horse-drawn carriage, greeting residents on the way with a very loud booming voice. Possibly this was his normal tone as Mrs Barnett, who was chairman of the local Women's Institute in the 1930s, was hard of hearing.

There was considerable land attached to Westwood House, some of which was given over to orchards. During the Second World War Mr Barnett is said to have had the fruit ready for sale in old bushel baskets.

MISCELLANEOUS FEATURES

There are two wall letter-boxes in Tilehurst which have been there since at least 1900, one opposite the church in Church Cottages and one at the Horncastle end of

The War Memorial soon after it was put up in 1920.

New Lane Hill. There is also a Victorian pillar-box at World's End on Bath Road. This is opposite the end of Burghfield Road and must at one time have been very isolated. As the recently closed Post Office was the only building bearing a sign stating the name, World's End now seems lost forever.

The War Memorial Cross was erected in 1920, originally at the point of The Triangle, facing down School Road. In the late 1960s it was moved onto the main grassed area of The Triangle when the part of Church Road passing behind The Triangle was removed. The area was pedestrianized in 1974 when the Memorial was moved again to its present, more central position on The Triangle.

CHAPTER SIX

Churches and Chapels

ANGLICAN CHURCHES

St Michael's Church

Of all the churches in Tilehurst St Michael's Church has a special place, partly because of its age, partly because of its architecture and partly because of the parish system and the Established Church.

In the 1100s visiting brethren would have come out to cut furze from Tilehurst Heath to cart back to Reading Abbey. These frequent visits eventually led to a church being built, probably of wood, which was dedicated to St Michael. It is probable that several buildings have been added to the original church. Part of the present Lady Chapel dates from around the thirteenth or fourteenth century, when there was just a nave and south aisle.

In the 1700s the structure was described as 'so ruinous in the walls and roof that it is in the utmost danger of falling'. Whether it was rebuilt or repaired at this stage is

St Michael's Church with ivy growing all up the tower. (C 2945. The Rural History Centre, University of Reading)

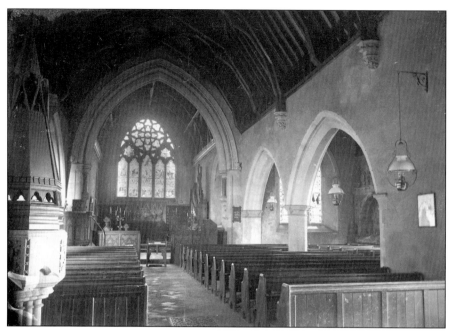

The interior of St Michael's Church, *c.* 1930.

not recorded. The tower was added in the 1730s with a ring of six bells, to which two trebles were added in 1885. A note of 1770 gives 'new pew the whole church except the pew that belong to John Blagrave Esq'.

The church fell into a state of disrepair again and in 1854 G.E. Street, the Diocesan Architect of Oxford from 1852 to 1856, was engaged to oversee major restoration work which was paid for entirely by the Routh family. The north aisle was added in 1855 by Revd John Routh, nephew of Dr Martin Routh.

Two stained glass windows are of particular note. The East Window of the Lady Chapel was designed by William Morris, the strong colours and the unique shell design backing the window indicating that it was one of his earlier designs. The East Window of the Chancel, which is by Wailes of Newcastle, depicts scenes from the life of Jesus, relating them to scenes from the Old Testament and including St Michael and St George. The south aisle contains a brass of Gauwin More and his wife, Isabella, both of whom died in 1469. Also of note is a large monument to Sir Peter Vanlore. Around the walls and on the ground in the churchyard and cemetery are graves and memorials to many of the notable figures of Tilehurst through the years.

At the centenary of Street's restoration work considerable alterations were made, but since then little has been done apart from regular maintenance and the addition to the north side of a Parish Centre, completed in 1993.

The Rectory was built in the 1800s and is now incorporated into Iris Court. In the time of Revd John Routh it housed his wife and their three daughters, along with some of their servants, possibly the cook and the housemaid, although they also had a footman, a kitchen maid, an under housemaid and a gardener. The large garden

The Sunday School boys at the Old National School, 1909.

had a lawn of sufficient size for fêtes, sports days and plays, all of which were very much a part of village life, particularly during the Second World War.

The Rectory was sold in 1967 to James Butcher Housing for the Elderly, and a more practical replacement was built on part of the original Rectory grounds. The church hall was also built on land belonging originally to the Rectory. It was opened in 1960.

When the Old National School was no longer used as a school, it was taken over by the Church and became known as Church House. As it was situated very much in the centre of the village it became a focal point not just for church activities, but for many other local functions.

In the 1900s there were mission halls in Kentwood, Little Heath and Calcot which eventually became the churches of St Mary Magdalen, St Catherine of Siena and St Birinus. These were all daughter churches of St Michael until each became a parish church in its own right.

St George's Church

In 1880 a temporary iron church was put up for troops living in Reading Barracks who wanted their own garrison church, and for people in the neighbouring community. St George's Church was eventually consecrated in 1886 when it was rebuilt in red brick in the Early English style. It has a chancel, north aisle and turret. It was originally part of Tilehurst but was taken over by Reading in 1889. The cemetery is situated some way from the church near the bottom of Norcot Road.

THE BAPTIST CHURCH

Tilehurst Free Church

Tilehurst Free Church is a comparative newcomer to the town. Over the years a lot of land all around the area has been bought for housing developments. One builder, Charles Gill, had developed the area along The Meadway and St Michael's Road but had an odd piece of land remaining. In 1941 he gave the land in Trust to the Reading Baptist Council. The council did not develop the land immediately, however, and for the next twenty years it was still necessary to travel across Reading to the Wycliffe Baptist Church, although several smaller meetings were held. In 1952 a couple from London set up a Bible study group in their new home in Park Lane in the evenings, and a local teacher started a Sunday school, which met in The Triangle Youth Centre. These people wanted to build an evangelical church based in Tilehurst, and in 1961 Tilehurst Free Church (Baptist) was built, part of the preparation of which involved dealing with a pond full of frogs in the grounds of The Priory. The church was officially opened in 1963.

THE METHODIST CHURCH

John Wesley is reported to have visited the area several times in the eighteenth century, a small chapel in Chapel Hill being used as a meeting place by the Reading Evangelical Society in 1797. The first open air services are reported to have been held around 1861 on a triangle of land in front of The Red Barn at School Road, now The Triangle. Local people were invited to attend and it is reported that the landlady of 'The Little Plough' accepted the invitation and arrived with her Wesleyan hymn

One of the earliest chapels was along this hill, which was subsequently called Chapel Hill, *c.* 1910.

The Methodist Church around the turn of the century.

book. In winter the 'open-air' congregation began to use a cottage called Sunnyside on the north side at the top of Norcot Hill. A Bible, reading desk, hymn books and a few seats were purchased. Afternoon and evening services were held here until the owners retired and needed to use the cottage as a residence again, and the congregation had to move on.

A coach house and stable were then loaned to the group, and they continued there using these premises not only for services but also for educational purposes.

At the time, a non-denominational evangelical chapel had already been erected in School Road in Tilehurst. Made of corrugated iron, it was run by a group of Trustees who had in their number several members of the Liebenrood family and Martin John Sutton, Mayor of Reading at the time. They offered this iron building to the Methodist Church on reasonable terms, which were settled in 1884.

As Tilehurst developed so the need for a more permanent brick building was felt, and the foundation stone for such was laid in 1904, with the church opening in 1905. The iron building was moved to the rear of the church building by volunteers. Members continued to use it for many years as a hall, kitchen, Sunday school and for many other activities.

The Oxford Road minister was responsible for Tilehurst Methodist Church at that time, and came to take weekday services and classes, while local preachers took the Sunday services.

The church saw several changes during this time. The Methodist Guild was started in 1908. A gallery was built in the church in 1931 to take a pipe organ, which would replace the original organ, and to provide extra seating, and an additional wooden building was erected to accommodate the expanding Sunday school. In 1934 the church finally got its own minister, who started the Boys' Brigade in the area.

Further development in the Kentwood Hill area of Tilehurst led to a second Methodist church being built. Around 1935 open air meetings were being held in that part of Tilehurst and a house in Coniston Drive was rented. Thanks to a gift from Arthur Newbery of a piece of land adjoining Newbury Park, however, the Methodist Church was able to build Kentwood Church, which opened in 1937.

In 1939 'People's Services' were started at Tilehurst Methodist Church, with handbills being distributed inviting people to attend. As an incentive, seats were reserved until 6.25 p.m. for anyone bringing a handbill. Regular members had to queue until that time before taking a seat, if there was room left.

During the Second World War a Christian 'Commando Campaign' was recalled as a particular time of spiritual uplift. Church buildings were made available to schools as their numbers grew because of the many evacuees. The popularity of a youth centre grew and it eventually became non-denominational.

After the war still more space was needed for the young people. Triangle House was built with the generous support of local tradespeople and good friends and supporters. It opened in 1946 and could accommodate over 100 people. It had a stage and there were activities on every day of the week. There was a 'Milk Bar' and popular concerts were held on Saturdays, with local talent and fellowship for all at a cost of 6d. Outside there was a hard tennis court, alongside which the Boys' Brigade practised their drill.

By 1956 the corrugated iron hall behind the church was totally inadequate. Triangle House was sold and the construction of new accommodation began, with a small hall, kitchen and toilets. In 1965 the new main hall was opened, and three more rooms and additional toilets were added in 1975, replacing a large wooden hut which was sold to the local Scout troop. A new organ was purchased for the church in 1967, the removal of the old one creating more space in the gallery for seating. In 1979 the Church celebrated the 75th anniversary of its original building.

THE UNITED REFORM CHURCH

In the late 1700s and early 1800s Revd Archibald Douglas had come from Broad Street Chapel in Reading and had organized meetings in surrounding villages. It is thought he used the same chapel on Chapel Hill as the Methodists had done before him, and launched the Evangelical Society in the area. In 1835 Mr Richard Woodeson, a shopkeeper at Armour, erected a new building in Armour Road, where No. 66 now stands. This new Congregational Church building was said to be very plain, furnished with wooden forms as seats and a pulpit at one end with two or three steps up to it, and lit by candles. There was no organ or other form of musical instrument. The preachers came from Reading mostly on foot, and so the 'Preacher's Beer', mentioned in the records at a cost of eight pence, must have been very welcome! Later records indicate a payment for the stabling of preachers' horses.

The church continued under the authority of the Broad Street Chapel in Reading until numbers grew and new accommodation was sought.

The United Reformed Church in Armour Road, with the brick water tower clearly visible, *c.* 1905.

In 1886 a document shows that negotiations were taking place with the Liebenrood family. The Church was hoping that the family would donate a parcel of land from its estate on which it could construct a new church building. The document states that the new church would be built of iron at a cost of £1,182. The negotiations were carried out by Walter John Brain, co-founder of Brain and Brain, Solicitors, and the Secretary of the Broad Street Chapel. In the event a brick and stone building was decided on and the memorial stone was laid in 1888 by Mr George Palmer, JP.

In 1889 the new Congregational Chapel was completed in Tilehurst and the old building was taken over for a time by the Salvation Army. At the same time there was a proposal to sell the chapel in Chapel Hill to help cover the cost of the new building. The *Reading Observer* wrote that the sermon preached by Revd Fairbairn, Principal of Mansfield College, Oxford, at the inaugural event was 'of great beauty and pathos and produced a marked impression on the crowded audience, who for an hour listened to the eloquent teaching of one of the ablest divines in England'. Tea was provided in the Wesleyan Chapel which had been kindly lent, but it was too small for the hundreds who sought refreshment which had to be supplied in two 'detachments'.

It is interesting to note what the press reported about the chairman of the meeting that evening:

> He was very glad that night to take the chair as a representative of those who took that broad view of the Christian Church. He was glad to know that Tilehurst were not following in the steps of Coley. Coley represented part of the town where ignorance and wrong were as great as in any other part, and if they went down there they would find three or four sections of religious thought who were not so much fighting the common enemy, sin, as they were fighting each other as to who should have the pre-eminence of teaching

the people right. Unfortunately the Church of England, who held the other end of Tilehurst parish, had allowed the people in that part to have it perhaps too much their own way. Therefore he considered that those connected with the chapel were really the Church of Tilehurst.(Laughter)

Further records relate that in 1892 'It was agreed that a proper chair be provided for the organist without delay'. And in 1898 that 'the policeman was to be asked to use his persuasive powers to stop the nuisance of boys running about the Chapel grounds'.

In 1905 attendance at the Sunday school was recorded at well over 100, as it was at the Band of Hope meeting during the week. A year later the school hall was built to accommodate these large numbers.

In 1915 records mention for the first time a 'New Independent Congregational Church in Tilehurst' which became affiliated to the Congregational Union. Between 1920 and 1924 new choir seating was installed, and a pipe organ acquired. Records state that 'Master Harold Padley appointed "blower" and to be paid an honorarium of £1 per annum'.

From 1925 to 1927 electric lighting was installed and new railings were erected around the buildings.

The first Manse was purchased in 1923 but was found to be unsuitable so a new Manse was erected in Westwood Road.

A vestibule in the front of the church was added to celebrate the centenary of the church in 1935.

The Scheme of Union was adopted by the Assemblies of the Congregational Church in England and Wales and the Presbyterian Church of England in 1972. The scheme contained the provisions necessary for the formation of the United Reformed Church.

THE ROMAN CATHOLIC CHURCH

St Joseph's Church

In the early days, people from Tilehurst who wished to attend the Catholic Church had to travel all the way to the Church of the English Martyrs on the corner of Tilehurst Road and Liebenrood Road.

This church was founded in 1926. The new modern church was built in 1976; the original church is now used as a hall. There had been plans to build a more local church in Tilehurst near the corner of Romany Lane with Norcot Road, but eventually some land was used which had been given some time before by a Mr Capelli, and St Joseph's Church was built in 1956 on the corner of Berkshire Drive with Park Lane. The project was much helped by Father William Kirk, who had started a football pools scheme which, over a period of twenty years, had raised enough money to build St Joseph's Church. The 8 a.m. service was moved to start twenty minutes later to accommodate many people who caught the one bus which came from Norcot on a Sunday morning. Ten years later St Joseph's became a separate parish with its own priest.

The shops in Park Lane, looking to the corner where St Joseph's Church now stands, *c.* 1940. (C L77/9. The Rural History Centre, University of Reading)

CHAPELS

In the late 1700s to early 1800s there were several Independent Nonconformist Chapels in Tilehurst. The maps and directories indicate one at the lower end of New Lane Hill, another near the water tower in Park Lane and another in Westwood Row. The one of most significance, however, was in Chapel Hill.

In 1797 this small chapel was taken over by the Reading Evangelical Society after several visits by John Wesley, the founder of Methodism. It was later converted into two cottages and eventually demolished around 1975, a new house being built on the site.

A directory lists Primitive Methodist and Wesleyan Chapels in the area in 1887.

CHAPTER SEVEN

Charities

ALMSHOUSES

Mary Lyne Almshouses, which can be found at the lower end of New Lane Hill, were endowed in 1851 by Mary Lyne of Burghfield for:

> six widows without encumbrances, or unmarried, of 60 years or upwards, belonging to the Church of England and of respectable character. Three to be chosen from Burghfield and three from Tilehurst.

As the area developed and parish boundaries changed the requirement remained, although the division of numbers changed to two from Burghfield, two from Theale and two from Tilehurst. In 1894 it was reported that 'Theale has one nomination in three . . . no one has been elected over the last 30 years'.

The Almshouses at the bottom of New Lane Hill.

Considering the hill leading up from the almshouses, some of the rules seem quite tough:

> The almswomen should, unless prevented by illness . . . attend divine service in the parish church of Tilehurst twice at least on every Sunday and once on every other day throughout the year on which morning service should be performed in that parish church . . .

The Tudor chimneys are a feature of the fine building.

BLAGRAVE RECREATION GROUND

In 1894 John Henry Blagrave gave a piece of land to the churchwardens and overseers of Tilehurst with the restriction that it should be:

> an open public playground for children and youths of the parish under the age of 14, that no building should be built on it other than a cricket or football pavilion of ornamental design, that no malt or spirituous liquors should be kept or sold on the land, and that the trustees should maintain the fences.

The ground was transferred to the Parish Council in 1898 who were soon reporting 'wilful damage to the pavilion, trees, pump and swings'. It was taken over by Reading Council in 1913 and was made smaller when a nursery school was built on part of the site during the Second World War. An ARP post still remains within the ground.

CHURCH LANDS

Records of this charity in Tilehurst go back as far as 1539. By the mid-1500s a William Fettiplace had laid claim to the piece of land adjacent to Tilehurst cemetery, parishioners had already built two almshouses, one church house, one house for the clerk of the parish, one smith's forge and two other houses.

Over the years there was further controversy as to who owned the land and properties, but it was finally resolved that as any profits from the rent were for the 'profit and ease of the whole parish' they came under the control of trustees.

The first two cottages, however, were pulled down in 1850, the smith's forge fell down in 1870 with materials from it being used for repairs, and the remaining dwellings became untenantable in 1878.

The Charity Commissioners report of 1906 states that three cottages had been reconstructed and the fourth had a parish room erected beside it. These four cottages, now known as Church Cottages, remain opposite St Michael's Church and are still run by trustees from that church.

THE NATIONAL SCHOOL

Revd Thomas Sheppard DD, who died in January 1814, gave £20 a year out of his own estate to establish a school in Theale. By 1837 no school had yet been

Church Cottages opposite St Michael's Church, *c.* 1910.

The Triangle with The Old National School beyond The Plough Inn.

established and it was proposed to build a school in Tilehurst instead, with Revd Thomas Sheppard's bequest as a basis. His widow offered to build the schoolhouse at her own expense and endowed it with a yearly sum of £16 10s 6d. An annual benefaction was also to be paid 'for ever' by Magdalen College, Oxford, and the school was also to be supported by other charitable subscriptions.

The Report of the Charity Commissioners of 1906 indicates that the school was conducted as an elementary school, going by the name of the Tilehurst National School. From 1905 the managers of the school allowed the Local Education Authority to use the school until the new 'provided' school was open, this being Park Lane School. As the school was no longer 'voluntary' Magdalen College was no longer required to make annual payments (see Chapter Eight)

POORS LAND

A report of 1906 states that, in 1786, a William Bellinghurst possessed some land in Burghfield from which 3s 4d was paid yearly by a man named Burton for the benefit of the poor of Tilehurst. The report, however, implies that the amount had not been paid for many years.

Similarly a person named Knapp gave £10 to be kept for 'a stock', the interest from which was to be distributed to the poor of Tilehurst. In 1786, however, the sum was said to be 'lost'.

Revd Dr Chandler recorded that after 1731 a charity of the yearly produce of £1 10s had been left by a Mr Wheat for three 'great coats' to be given to the poor of Tilehurst. The money came from an estate in Silchester, which was then the property of Mr Lyford, surgeon of Basingstoke. In 1897 eight coats costing £4 9s had been distributed. In 1906 30s a year had been given to the clergyman, who purchased two 'great coats' for two poor men of Tilehurst selected by him. They are later described in the 1906 report as 'reefer coats for aged men who are past work'. This charity was eventually absorbed into the Poors Land Charity, which still exists today.

Several parcels of land were deemed to be for the benefit of the poor and were enclosed by an Act of Parliament in 1817. Over 9 acres adjoining the workhouse and a further 3 acres on Kentwood Common were leased from 1816 to John Webb who paid a rent of £17 4s annually. Sophia Sheppard rented the remaining 15 acres on Kentwood Common near Harmour, paying a rent of £26 7s. The Trustees were John Blagrave, as lord of the manor, along with the Rector, the churchwardens and overseers of the poor. About 220 families benefited from the proceeds of this charity when about 4 cwt coal was bought for them in the winter months. A small reserve of money was kept in case of sickness of any poor persons.

Should any of the land not be let then it was to be planted with furze wood or cutting fuel which would then also be used for the poor. Should there be more money than was needed for fuel then it was left to the discretion of the Trustees to use it in other ways for the benefit of the poor.

By 1906 the lord of the manor was Mr Henry Barry Blagrave, but neither he nor the Rector at this time played any further part in the administration of the charity, which was now left to the churchwardens and overseers. The land had been divided up and is now described as:

The 1913 Health Crusade in Victoria Recreation Ground.

Another gathering by Victoria Recreation Ground.

8 acres near Park Farm, Church End let to R. Blagrave. Land on the common at Tilehurst which was let in allotments to different tenants. Land at Chapel Hill and Harmour Hill similarly. Land on the common let to F. Wilder and other trustees for a public recreation ground. Land on Tilehurst Common let to Richard Armstrong.

The allotments were let in sections of 20 perches (about 16½ metres), and the only outgoings were for occasional fencing. The income from the allotments was used to buy coal which was distributed at Christmas and it is noted in the aforementioned report that in 1904 the exceptional amount of 64 tons and 16 cwt was distributed in 4 cwt portions. People were deemed to be poor if the annual value of their household was not more than £10. There were around 200 such households in Tilehurst and 100 in Theale.

Many transactions must have taken place as land was disposed of for building, and the Victoria Recreation Ground was taken over by Reading Council in 1914, although it still pays an annual rent. The allotments behind the ground are still in the possession of the Poors Land Charity where there are some 100 holdings. Proceeds from the rent money from the allotments are distributed by the present Trustees, although not now in the form of coal, to those whose application fulfils the objects of the scheme.

THE VILLAGE HALL

The Liebenrood family donated the land for the Village Hall, which was built in 1893 and could accommodate 350 people. It was originally intended to be used by 'working men' as a library, with copies of the daily papers, and for lectures. However, the first meeting of the Parish Council was held there too, and, later, ratepayers' meetings. The Parish Council tried to take over the hall completely in 1901 but did not succeed. Over the years, it has been run by a succession of trustees, who have had to maintain the proviso that no alcoholic liquor should be sold, and that no views other than Christian should be taught there. It is still very well used by the community for a whole variety of purposes.

THE WORKHOUSE

There was a workhouse for the poor in Tilehurst from about 1767. A map of 1870 shows not only an area known as Workhouse Copse but also the Old Workhouse situated back from the road but approximately opposite the end of City Road, where Park Farm later stood. The farmhouse which had been the poor house was demolished in the late 1960s.

Paupers in the area were grouped into categories: those able to work, those who were infirm and those under the age of ten. Some forty people could be housed. The numbered rooms were very sparsely furnished with a bedstead, a flock or feather bed and bolster, a pair of sheets and a blanket. Some rooms had a coffer or a rug or stool. Fifteen spinning wheels were also available.

In 1781 the committee passed a resolution that:

in future no person above the age of 16 shall receive any punishment but by signed order of the committee for the time being which order shall be entered in their book stating the offence for which such punishment was ordered and that persons under that age may be punished at the discretion of the Master by flogging so that at one time no more than six stripes be inflicted by a common Birch Rod and that the punishment be inflicted before the rest of the children.

Also that 'on no pretence whatever [may] any clog or fetter be fastened to the limb of any person belonging to the Home'.

The inmates were paid out of the Poor Rate, but in 1795 the Berkshire Justices added a supplement to their wage based on the price of bread, hence the beginning of the 'bread lists'. In 1805 the price of a gallon loaf was 2s 3d.

In 1802 all the poor of the parish had to be inoculated with cow-pock in order to protect them from small-pox which was rife at the time. The Parish paid for this at 5s per person.

The overseers of the Parish had to inspect the workhouse regularly, and also had to 'pay paupers weekly and make sure the poor receive due attention'.

In 1827 Richard Rivers was Governor of the Poor House where he is reported to 'farm the poor at 4s per head per week'. He had the responsibility of teaching the inmates the simple craft of weaving and he took prayers night and morning.

By 1842 the Parish had to 'take into consideration the propriety of letting, selling or otherwise disposing of the Poor House'. Notice was sent out to ratepayers that it was valued at £598 18s 9d. Bradfield Union sold the property in 1843. A resident relates a story passed on by her mother that when a neighbour had to go to the workhouse his dog was destroyed. When his family went to visit him he could only meet them at the gate where they were able to pass little gifts through the railings to him. When he died he left just a case with his watch in it.

CHAPTER EIGHT

Education and Childhood

Many schools have operated in the Tilehurst area over the years. Most children in Tilehurst would walk to school along the rough roads with wide and dirty ditches; a few came by bicycle. Illnesses were a constant problem and would quickly reach epidemic proportions. Fleas were rampant; most mothers went through their children's hair before they left for school as it was considered a disgrace to have fleas. Children dreaded catching them, although they found it a constant source of entertainment in class to watch fleas on others. Medals would be awarded for proficiency and attendance. Initially it was more important for the children to achieve a certain grade or standard. Children of mixed ages would therefore be taught together until they had reached the required standard to move up, rather than moving up year by year by age. Some would attend the same class several times before actually leaving the school. Many children left school at fourteen to start work the very next day.

THE NATIONAL SCHOOL

The National School was the earliest recorded school of note in Tilehurst. It was built in 1819 by Mrs Sophia Sheppard of Amport, Hants, sister of Dr Martin Routh, then Rector of Tilehurst, who donated the land. Mrs Sheppard settled a small annual income towards the upkeep of the school through Magdalen College, Oxford. It was also supported by charitable subscriptions. The school provided education for the children who did not attend one of the small private schools that were run in the area, many of which ran for only a short period, with numbers ranging from thirty-seven to just two pupils. There was obviously a need for such a school as children as old as eleven were coming who had never attended school before. A small weekly charge was made. Although it started as a primary school, an infant school was added later and the establishment became known to many as the National School.

The building itself was quite large, with a main entrance that led to a large school hall on the left with cloakrooms behind. There were a couple of small rooms in the centre and then a smaller hall on the right, where cookery and laundry classes were subsequently held. Behind and on the first floor of the central part was private living accommodation for the caretaker. There was a garden in the front of the school, but only a small walled garden at the back.

There were two carved stones on the wall inside the main hall, which bore a beautifully carved coat of arms relating the story of the school. The inscriptions read: 'On land given by the Rector this school was erected by Sophia, Widow of Thomas Sheppard D.D. of Amport, Hants MDCCCXIX' and 'This building was erected by Sophia, widow of Thomas Sheppard DD of Amport in the County of Hants on land

Part of the Old National School used as an assembly point for a Girl Guide parade, 1968.
(*The Reading Evening Post*)

given by the Rector of Tilehurst for the use of a National School to be supported by charitable subscriptions and by annual benefaction of £36.10.00 to be paid to the Rector and his successors forever by Magdalen College in Oxford. The cost of keeping this building in good repair is to be defrayed out of the above benefaction. MDCCCXIX.' Sadly, these stones have been destroyed.

In 1872 there were seventy-six pupils on the register with a headteacher, a sewing mistress, an assistant and a pupil teacher. The log book of that year shows that some families were finding it difficult to pay the fees and were only going to be allowed one week in arrears. Attendance was very irregular, particularly at harvest time and because of illness. Whooping cough, diphtheria, smallpox and scarlet fever all took their toll. During an outbreak of diphtheria in 1876, which cost the lives of several children, the water was tested and found to be polluted. It was recommended that proper drainage was used instead of slop drainage into a ditch.

Excesses of weather could also affect attendance. As many children walked to school and went home at lunch time, when the weather was very hot some would not bother to return for afternoon school. If there was bad snow it would have been difficult to walk to school, and travel by some other means, horse and cart for example, would have been no easier because of the hills.

Attendance was also affected by a fair in Reading or a fête at Theale, and by the many outings that the Sunday School seemed to organize during the school week. Sometimes numbers dropped so low that the school was closed for all or part of the day. Some of the boys only attended on a part-time basis as they worked, illegally, in Norcot potteries.

The school was described as being very dark with the windows high up, but the children were well looked after on the whole and if they attended regularly they were given a suit by the Rector.

At one time an evening school was held when the basics were taught. An entry from the log book reads: 'Agricultural worker left school at 12, now 21 allowed to progress with subtraction.'

It had been the intention to close the school on 31 March 1905, as the tenancy of the land at the back of the school would then expire and could not be renewed. However, the sub-committee of the education committee arranged to rent the school from the trustees, temporarily paying a rent of 10s per annum. By 1908 it was let rent free for educational purposes.

In its final years the Old National School was renamed Norcot Temporary Council School and was still used by children attending Park Lane or Norcot School for practical classes. From 1920 the girls would walk to the Old National School for their cookery and laundry classes, which were taken by a teacher who came up from Reading. The girls had cookery one week and laundry the next, many expecting to become servants when they left. Laundry lessons consisted of washing one day and ironing the next; the flat irons were heated on a gas stove. All these lessons were conducted in silence. The teacher was said to be very bad tempered because she suffered from indigestion – one hopes it was not caused by having to sample what her pupils had cooked!

The Old National School closed as a school in 1912. The buildings were used for a time by St Michael's Church as a Sunday school and for other church activities, and it came to be known as Church House. Soup and bread were provided there at lunch times for the children of families who could not afford to eat. It was eventually demolished in 1968; a small plaque on the side of a shop in School Road near The Plough Inn records where it stood. Part of the surrounding wall of the school can still be found incorporated into the wall at the rear of the National Westminster Bank.

BOARD SCHOOLS

In 1878 the Tylehurst School Board was formed to investigate the high incidence of truancy. They found that 108 children were attending school, some going to Reading, Sulham, Englefield and Purley as well as Tilehurst, but 82 children were not attending any school. They were either roaming the streets or were illegally employed in the potteries and on the farms. Several schools, Grovelands, Park Lane and Norcot Council, were set up as board schools, which were run by an elected committee or a board of governors. There was initially a charge for attending such schools which worked on a sliding scale, farmers children being charged 4d and farm labourers 2d, but this was abolished in 1891.

Grovelands School

Grovelands Board School was built on the corner of Craig Avenue with Oxford Road near the end of Grovelands Road in 1880. It was opened in December of that year for 500 children, with a charge of 2*d* for each child weekly, payable in advance. The log book for January 1884 reads:

> The Barracks children have been kept away on account of our having children from Tilehurst Common, and I have, with the cognisance of the Manager, asked the Tilehurst children to stay away until it is safe for them to come back.

The Tilehurst children returned a fortnight after the Barracks children were re-admitted. Unfortunately no further details are known about this story.

Grovelands School was eventually taken over by Reading Council, although during the First World War it was linked with Norcot School as its own building was used as a hospital. At the time Battle Hospital was the Workhouse, and about fifty patients from there were transferred to Grovelands School. (Battle became the primary War Hospital, taking survivors from the massacre of the Somme.) The two schools shared facilities at the Norcot site, with that school operating on a half-day basis as a result. Some Tilehurst children also went to Wilson Central School, and part of that too was taken over as a war hospital. Other suitable buildings, such as the Old National School and church halls, had to be commandeered for school use as there were so many children to accommodate.

Children from Tilehurst who attended Grovelands used to go to school in the morning (9 a.m. to 1 p.m.) in the summer and in the afternoon (1.30 p.m. to 5.30 p.m.) in the winter so that Grovelands children could get home in the light.

Park Lane School

Park Lane School opened in 1890, and from then until 1902 was known as the Tylehurst Board School. It took children up to the age of fourteen. Children were coming into the school aged as old as eight, nine and even ten having had no previous education. It seems that there were fifty-six boys and fifty-six girls, with a teacher in charge of the infants and the head teacher, Mr Edwin Jones, teaching all the rest. The school also took many children from gipsy families when they were in the area, usually along Chapel Hill.

Revd John Routh made several visits within the first few months of the school opening and expressed his satisfaction. He presumably missed the entry in the log book of 4 October 1890 which states: 'Found several indications on the walls of WCs of the low moral tone of the children.'

In his first report to the school board the head teacher echoes the request of many other schools at that time in seeking a permanent teacher to take charge of Standard 1 and Standard 2. He also requested 'brushes as aids to cleanliness, and scales, weights and measures to practically teach arithmetic'. He finally drew the attention of the board 'to the marked difference in the condition of the children, some being from the local private schools, others driven in from the road, half-fed and half-clothed'.

At his next visit Revd John Routh was informed of the 'bad tone of the "City" children'. Later that month, even though the head teacher had sixty children of Standards III to VII in his charge, he examined Standards I and II for himself and found 'some of [the children] in a most deplorable state . . . and unable to read or write the simplest words'.

A little note of optimism appeared at the start of the next month, however: 'Improvement in tone, no soap stolen during previous month.'

In January 1891 the numbers attending Park Lane dropped dramatically because of measles and in the middle of February the school was closed completely until early March. No doubt it was a relief when the next term proceeded without too much trouble, ending on 31 July for five weeks' holiday.

The following term, however, did not start well because of a 'late and protracted harvest'. On 23 October it is recorded that 'many children [were] prevented from attending school owing to the floods'.

The report of January 1892 states that 'the Headmaster deserves much credit for the extent to which he has established good discipline. Unnecessarily hampered however by the want of promptitude in staffing the school in accordance to its growing needs.' In October of that year illness struck again, this time scarlet fever. A savings bank was started, and by December 'has developed beyond the most sanguine expectations. Number of depositors 147, amount deposited £50.18.6d.'

Further extracts from the log book give some idea of the day-to-day happenings at the school, and show how the life of the staff and pupils was affected by events both local and national:

June 1893: Many cases of sore throat – panic of diphtheria (Bills put up through parish started panic).

5 October 1894: Have group Standard 3 with Standard 4 to 7 since September 17 and am doing my best with them under my sole charge 101 on register.

1910

9 children were excluded by the medical officer on account of verminous head and 1 for ringworm.

Park Lane School, *c*. 1910.

18 March: 4 children taken off register, gone to Canada. This is the 4th or 5th family we have lost in this way lately.

9 May: A special address was made to the children on the death of King Edward Vll.

6 September: 3/6½ stolen from Masters desk during dinner hour.

25 October: 8 excluded because of mumps. Received instruction to prosecute Bert Richardson recently left school for wilful damage to school property. More stealing and breaking in – knife, rubbers, key, pencils, windows continually broken, stone from catapult, buttons cut off coats in cloakroom, sent for mother who strongly objected to her boy being punished.

1911

14 July: The heat has been extreme 84–86 degrees in school. Children and teachers alike have suffered.

24 July: School closed for Temperance and Congregational Sunday School treat.

16 September: Conducted a party of 29 children to Crystal Palace to Pageant of Empire.

1912

10 January: A dinner centre opened at the Old National School by the Borough Education Authority for feeding necessitous children. 26 from this school received tickets. . . . Rain and flooding prevents the attendance of many children.

26 January: The Reverend Cooper Smith distributed interest to children from savings in school bank. He also delegated the right to inflict corporal punishment in accordance to the Reading regulations.

1913

October: Another measles epidemic closed the school for 3 weeks.

1914

30 October: Sent off 23 pairs of woollen socks knitted by girls of school for use of soldiers at the front – cost of wool over £1 paid largely by the children.

6 November: Letter of thanks for above received from Lady in Waiting on behalf of H.M. the Queen.

1915

January: An outbreak of whooping cough lowered attendance at the school.

30 April: Children brought 6 doz new laid eggs for Reading Hospital for wounded soldiers.

1916

22 May: Daylight Saving Bill came into operation.

26 May: A few infants have not been up in time for morning school, but generally the earlier rising has made little difference.

22 September: Collection of vegetables from School gardens for prizes given by the Rector. All exhibits were afterwards sent to the Reading War Hospitals.

2 October: Reverted to Greenwich Time.

1917

13 March: Mr Heatherington absent this week on military duty.

11 May: Wilful mischief by a number of older boys stone throwing and breaking up things in school garden. These boys . . . have no fathers at home to keep them in order and they are beyond their mothers' control.

1918

22 January: Mrs Selwood granted leave of absence her husband being home from the front.

11–12 February: School closed. Teachers requisitioned to make our 'Ration Cards' in Reading. In addition to ordinary school plots of 40 poles, the boys will again cultivate an extra 20 poles as special war work for food production.

17 July: Mr Heatherington absent attending military medical examination.

4 December: Received stock ordered in July last, then sent but lost in transit.

1919

28 March: An accident happened at the school gardens this afternoon, a boy receiving a stab close to the eye from the point of a fork.

1 April: The boy died in the Royal Berkshire Hospital from septic poisoning. At the inquest on the 2nd April a verdict of accidental death was brought in and everyone concerned was exonerated from blame. The poor lad in turning quickly while stooping down brought himself into contact with the fork of another boy and so a slight puncture close to the right eye was caused. He was sent immediately to the Doctor who dressed the wound but septic poisoning set in with fatal results.

[Later the parents brought an action against Reading Corporation to recover damages as compensation for the death of their son. It was dismissed on the grounds that 'no negligence had been proved, but that there was abundant proof that the greatest care was taken in the conduct of these gardening classes. The Headmaster was again exonerated from any blame.']

19 July: Peace Celebrations 'Official Day' Treat in Prospect Park, tea, races etc.

23 July: Tilehurst Peace Celebrations. Service on Recreation Ground – sports, tea – a very fine treat. Extra weeks holiday in Summer.

1921

19 July: School outing to Southsea by charabancs with visit to the Victory. 76 took part. A most enjoyable and instructive outing, no mishaps of any kind.

School Road outside Park Lane School *c.* 1920.

1923

21 March: The boys have had to bring under cultivation a new plot of ground for school gardens their former gardens being taken for building purposes.

6 July: The heat of the past week has been intense – over 100 degrees inside school. Workmen have been hammering almost continuously so that work has been most trying.

1925

Both whooping cough and impetigo are reported during the year.

December: Complaint of bad quality of coal supply and large amount of dust and small in it all of which help to make our rooms very dirty. Temperature 42 degrees.

18 December: F.W. White resigned charge of school today.

During the 1940s Park Lane School had 'outposts' – classrooms in any public buildings available, often some distance from the main school building. They used the hall of the Old National School as a classroom, which the teacher described as 'grim and forbidding, large, lofty and dark'. They had a primitive stove in the winter with a guard around it. They also used the Methodist Youth Centre at The Triangle for two classes with just a curtain to separate them, one of the classrooms having the stage in it. Barclays Bank now stands on the site of the Youth Centre.

Many schools were involved in the 'Dig for Victory' campaign during the Second World War. There were allotments in Wardle Avenue to help the war effort, and the school children also helped out by stacking corn at Hall Place Farm in the summer. Children from both Park Lane and Norcot Schools used Victoria Recreation Ground for games, as neither school had its own playing fields, but both had areas that were cultivated for vegetables.

The old school warning road sign for The Laurels. (L77/11. The Rural History Centre, University of Reading)

The Laurels

In 1948 The Laurels opened as a school, initially as the infant department to Park Lane School. The building is over 200 years old, and was described as being on 'Tilehurst Heights'. When it was auctioned in 1910 it had four reception rooms and a room hall, ten bedrooms and dressing rooms, stabling and farmery, gardens, grounds and a paddock. It was privately occupied until 1939 when it became a First Aid Post for the Civil Defence throughout the war. It was subsequently purchased for Park Lane School from the executors of the former owner for £3,100.

Norcot Council School

By 1906 board schools had been abolished, the local council taking over the running of the schools. Norcot Council School was built in 1906, on the corner of Norcot Road with Blundells Road, at the other end of the village from Park Lane School. Mr Saxby was headmaster.

When Calcot Infants' School closed in that same year, the children were transferred to Norcot, and Mr Illsley the carrier would bring them up from Calcot. His horse pulled a covered cart which the children found very dark inside. They had to line up at Calcot to get on the cart, but at least then had the best seats before the carrier arrived at Horncastle to pick up some more children. The horse often had quite a job to pull that load up Cockney Hill. He would drop them off at Park Lane School first then go on to Norcot School, but they all had to walk down the hill to Calcot at the end of the day. Once children reached the age of eight they could no longer use the transport but had to walk. They came up together and were nearly always late.

Classes were conducted at Norcot with the children sitting at double desks made of iron with a bench on a hinge so that it would tip up. There was a groove in the desk top to take pencils, and an inkwell. The desks were ranged in rows on tiers, with the lowest standard at the front for the lazy and naughty ones, and the highest standard at the back. With such large classes, regularly over fifty pupils, it was the only way to keep control.

In 1925–6 Norcot and Park Lane Schools were reorganized. The juniors went to Park Lane and the seniors to Norcot. In 1938 the Parish Council decided that there was no possibility of extending the school if there were to be considerable housing developments in the Tilehurst area, and another site had to be found for new playing fields. However, the outbreak of the Second World War prevented the plans from progressing any further.

Mr Saul was appointed headmaster in 1940 and was reputed to be very strict. This was probably a good thing as during this time the population of the school exploded with large numbers of evacuees being admitted. Nearly all Tilehurst families were asked to provide billets for evacuees, most of the children coming from West Hill Girls' School, Putney, and schools in Canterbury. More space had to be found and lessons moved between the school and the church halls. Music lessons were taken at Park Lane School and assemblies on Fridays held at the Old National School.

In 1942 a meals kitchen was opened at the school and in 1947 prefabricated classrooms were ready for use. At the end of the war, all the children were given a pound of chocolate milk powder as a gift from Canada.

In 1945 swimming lessons were given at Scours Lane Baths, and Mrs Jordan was given leave of absence as her husband was coming home, having been a prisoner in Japan for over three years.

On 24 May 1946 a special play to celebrate Empire Day was enacted to the rest of the school and parents. 'Victory' sports were held in Palmer Park.

In 1947 a telephone was installed in the head teacher's room. Lorry loads of boys from the school worked for a week at a time at the Agricultural Camps at Kingston Bagpuize and East Hendred, and many visits were arranged to local industries for those children who would soon be leaving.

In 1948 senior girls played tennis at the Victoria Square Courts, and nine coaches took the whole school to Bognor Regis for their summer outing.

In 1949 four German children from Dusseldorf were admitted to Norcot School, and Mr Saul retired after forty-six years teaching in Tilehurst, the last ten as headmaster of Norcot Secondary Modern School.

In 1951 additional land was leased from the south side of the school, across the bridle path, for additional school gardens.

In 1955 there was another turn-about as the school was reorganized to become Norcot County Primary School. The schools were 'zoned' at this time and teachers were 'volunteered' to move from Park Lane to Norcot. It had been anticipated that

Norcot School, 1906.

Empire Day celebrations at Norcot School, 24 May 1915.

the school would be run down and closed at this time, but the rapid increase in the birth rate meant that the places were much needed – there were 243 children on the roll. Despite the changes, the school was not treated as a new school, and the primary children had to make do with equipment previously used by the secondary school. The hall was very narrow, a 'marching hall' to get from one class to another, but despite this it was used for assemblies, plays and so on. A motto remained on the wall: 'Do thy duty that is best, leave unto thy Lord the rest.'

It seemed that although Park Lane had moved on with the times, Norcot had remained rather more encapsulated, although a very happy school, serving the locality. School life continued to flourish, despite many ups and downs, until 1985, when there was considerable discussion concerning the future of the school as new, purpose-built schools were now in operation. In 1988 the school numbers fell and the school finally closed in 1989.

OTHER SCHOOLS

Calcot School

Calcot Infants' School, which was situated on Bath Road, opened in 1874 when fifteen children under the age of seven enrolled. Later that year a Sunday school was held in the same building between 2 p.m. and 4 p.m. The school was under the benefaction of John Henry Blagrave, and the reports about it were very favourable in

The original Calcot School with the bell tower.

the early years. Not only did Mr and Mrs Blagrave frequently visit the school, but they also provided the children with treats in the summer and at Christmas. They also distributed gifts and prizes on many occasions, and sometimes provided clothing. The school had several new head teachers over the years, the last change resulting in unexpectedly poor reports from the Inspectors. The school closed in 1906.

In 1937 fifty-seven children attended the new primary school in Calcot, this time on the site between Bath Road and Royal Avenue. The old building came into its own again when it was used as an annexe for two classes in 1956-7 while additional work was being carried out on the present school buildings.

The old school building was used as a mission hall before St Birinus Church was built, and at different times has been a county police house, a village hall, a Home Guard post and a polling station. It was finally put up for auction and sold to be converted into a private dwelling. The bell tower was removed, the bell itself going to St Birinus Church.

The Highlands School was started in 1929 in Wardle Avenue. In 1969 it became a Joint Educational Trust with St Edward's Boys Preparatory School. This private school is still functioning today.

Stoneham Boys School opened in 1955 and Westwood Girls in 1958; these merged in 1985 to become Prospect School. Other secondary schools opened including Littleheath in 1963, Meadway in 1971 and Denefield in 1976.

As Tilehurst expanded primary schools were opened, many later separating into junior and infant schools. St Michael's opened in 1956, Birch Copse and Churchend in 1962, Westwood Farm in 1963, Moorlands in 1966, Springfields in 1969, Upcroft and Ranikhet in 1974 and Downsway in 1975. The special school of Brookfields opened in 1974.

OUT OF SCHOOL ACTIVITIES

In the early part of this century children played out in the streets, just listening for the occasional horse and cart, and later the occasional car. After school, at the weekends and in the summer holidays some went to join their mothers willow stripping. There were rod beds for basket chairs down Langley Hill to Calcot and the Holy Brook area. Several times a year there would be a visiting fun fair which set up at the end of Chapel Hill.

The children would go tadpoling in the big pond at the back of The Bear Inn and in the winter the Broad Pool, which was close to where the water tower now stands, would freeze over so that it was possible to skate. It was quite dangerous, and also quite lonely as there were no houses up Langley Hill, just woods. Although there was plenty of rubbish there, children also played in the chalk pit off the end of Westwood Road and Chepstow Road. These and other activities must have proved rather distracting for the children as they walked to school, even though they risked punishment if they were late.

Some children had to work in the house before they were allowed out on Saturday mornings. Then they would join their friends for walks in the fields or woods, playing with whips and tops or hoops, or skipping. Some of the lads would play tick-

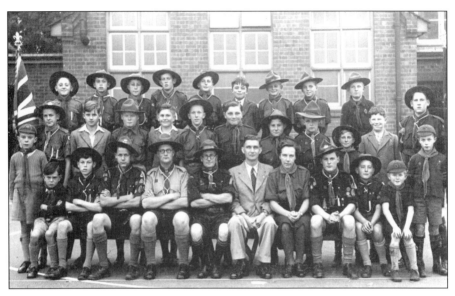

Tilehurst Scouts outside the Old National School, *c.* 1940.

tack with pieces of wood. At other times potatoes would be scrounged from home to bake on a fire, and one of the boys would bring his accordian for a sing-song. The children would climb trees, make camps and have fights, not that they could recall what they were about! More mischievous pranks involved tying together door knockers along Westwood Road, pulling the string and then running away!

In the evenings when it was dark, it was out with paper and pencils, or paints, or time for a quiz or spellings, then to bed by candle light.

Sunday afternoons was the time for family walks and there were miles of footpaths, which would take you anywhere but it would always be countryside. Each of the churches ran a Sunday school with treats and outings especially at Christmas and in the summer. The Boys' and Girls' Brigades were started in the 1930s.

Some Scouting had been started in the early 1900s although things floundered somewhat during the First World War as many of the leaders were called up. In 1929, however, a troop was started, sponsored by St Michael's Church. Sadly the Group Scoutmaster had to move away in 1932 to find work elsewhere during the depression. The group re-registered in 1936 when it used to meet in the Old National School. The scouts helped considerably during the Second World War, among other things distributing chocolate and cans of soup to evacuees as they queued at Park Lane School in 1939.

The 1st Tilehurst Guide Company was started in 1927, and, along with the Scout troop, founded the Tilehurst Eisteddfod in 1954 with an Arts and Crafts competition, in order to raise funds for a building. The event was held at Ranikhet Camp with Sir Felix Pole as President. It then moved to the Old National School, and is still held today, with many more attractions and at a variety of venues.

CHAPTER NINE

The War Years

THE FIRST WORLD WAR

In common with the whole of the country, Tilehurst suffered the distress and disruption of the First World War. The coming of mains drainage to the area coincided with the war, and some of the many problems of war-time are perhaps highlighted when one looks at the progress of this work. In 1913 Reading Council Minutes reported:

> the need for effectually draining the area has long been apparent and this need has recently been emphasised by evidence showing that in a number of cases domestic sewage is disposed of in gardens appurtenant to dwelling houses the water supply to which is derived from shallow wells situate in the same gardens.

The contractor had three tasks to accomplish:

1. A general drainage scheme to connect Tilehurst to the existing Borough scheme.
2. A surface water scheme to relieve roads of flooding during rainfall.
3. Lowering the subsoil water level of the district, which would be achieved by piercing the clay.

Considerable damage to land was expected. The burgesses met in the Village Hall and urged speed in doing the work. Although work did start in early 1914 and three gangs of men were operating around Polstead Road, Norcot Road, Chapel Hill, School Road and Westwood Road, some labour troubles were experienced. By September of that year a considerable number of men had been called up and only one gang remained. Although 'first class work' was reported as being done, there were problems in diverting the water; it was pointed out that men should be employed for agricultural purposes at that time, and there were considerable delays in delivering materials.

As work progressed so more households were asking for mains drainage, even though there were cases of claims for damage to land. Work was held up 'because of weather and war' and the contract extended.

By 1915 the contractor was able to report that items 2 and 3 had been completed with the 'resulting improvement in health far exceeding expectations', but the general drainage was not yet complete.

Come 1919 the ratepayers held a meeting, again in the Village Hall. The same contractor retendered to complete the work but then ran into more difficulties because of a railway strike, and an iron moulders strike, which caused delay in the manufacture of manhole covers. However, by 1921 the contract was completed. As Tilehurst continued to expand improved drainage was installed as each new development was built.

As a lot of men were called up, local shops were run mostly by the women. Girls who did not work in the shops often went into service.

What joy there must have been for everyone when the war ended. On Wednesday 23 July 1919 Peace Celebrations were held, with a service in Blagrave Recreation Ground between 1 and 2 p.m. followed by tea in Victoria Recreation Ground from 4.30 to 6 p.m. Then on 4 August 1919 Victoria Recreation Ground was closed to the public from 5 p.m. until dusk for entertaining the soldiers, although no bonfire was allowed.

After the war the Memorial Cross was set up on School Road. A local character known as 'Aunty Rose' regularly used to get a bucket of hot water and a scrubbing brush from the Old National School to scrub it clean.

THE SECOND WORLD WAR

During the Second World War the schools and churches of Tilehurst played their part and provided the community with strong leadership and a united purpose. Nearly all the households in the area took in evacuees. The only house at the top of Cockney Hill at that time had a hay loft where a mother and her three children stayed. Some evacuees stayed on after the war, married and settled in Tilehurst.

One lady organized working parties and managed to obtain a lot of material although from where no one was ever quite sure. The material was distributed to other ladies who made it into pyjamas, shirts, aprons and so on. A sale was held twice a year and orders were taken.

Plays were performed, which helped to take people's minds off their menfolk who

Norcot Junction with the Rex Cinema, c. 1940.

Left: Count John McCormack sings at the Red Cross concert, 1941. Right: William McIlroy addresses the crowds at the same concert. On the platform sit Lord Iliffe and Revd Francis Sherwood.

were away at war. The plays were rehearsed at Westwood House and performed on the Rectory lawn in the summer. Pantomimes were also performed and it must have seemed strange watching those during the summer months. They were so popular though that years after the war two Christmas pageants were held, which had a cast of some 150 people and were performed on The Triangle, using the Plough as the inn in Bethlehem and having gifts from Warings the bakers and Stevens the butcher. It is said that the audience stood four deep and all the costumes were made out of practically nothing, mostly bits from jumble sales.

A tent was put up in the Rectory ground by the YMCA for the entertainment of troops from Ranikhet Camp. Nightly concerts were held here until a permanent hut was built at the camp, and ladies were on duty all day to serve hot drinks, sandwiches and cakes. One imagines that such occasions would have been quite moving for Revd Francis Sherwood, the Rector of St Michael's Church at the time, as one of his sons was killed and another taken prisoner of war.

Other voluntary social committees were all active in raising funds for war charities including the Red Cross, TocH and the ARP (Air Raid Precaution). In 1941 a big concert was held at which the Irish tenor John McCormack sang, and the Band of the Royal Berkshire Regiment played. Also present on that occasion were Lord Iliffe and William McIlroy, then Mayor of Reading, along with some 1,600 people. There was community singing of many of the favourite wartime songs. At the end of the evening £120 had been raised for the Red Cross.

Ranikhet Camp

In 1940 Ranikhet Camp, able to accommodate over 1,000 people, was built quickly on a large expanse of land stretching from Church End Lane and taking in the area now bounded by Combe Road, Poole Close, Elvaston Way and Stanham Road. The camp was called Ranikhet after a hill station used by the Royal Berkshire Regiment when it was stationed in northern India in the 1920s. As this new camp was built on a hill and away from the barracks, it was an appropriate name.

A rather tongue in cheek entry which appeared in the Regimental magazine at the time reads:

> Somewhere in the wilds of England a new hutted camp is gradually taking shape. Seen some months ago the site appeared to have survived an intensive bombardment during the last war and never to have recovered, indeed the name of the adjoining height 'Lousehill' seemed particularly appropriate since the huts have appeared at all sorts of queer angles, this by design to defeat the hun who presumably is expected to look for the normal neat and ordered lines. The accommodation is being taken over as fast as it is ready . . . parade ground has yet to appear but there are good training grounds which reproduce conditions on the front consisting of mud and water.

Men who had been called up for service were initially billeted around Reading until Ranikhet became the Primary Training Centre for the ten week basic training before the men were sent on to Blandford Camp. Troops from the Royal Berkshire

The United States Airmen join in the Remembrance Day service.

Regiment returned to the camp for rehabilitation after seeing action in Flanders in 1940. The History of the Royal Berkshire Regiment reports that:

> they returned to their own country, and went into Ranikhet Camp at Tilehurst. Reading welcomed them with open arms, and provided them with a warmth of greeting that was to prove an inspiration in the reconstruction of the battalion. Everyone felt that they had come home.

Local residents accommodated wives who came to visit their husbands there.

Military training exercises continued with the defence of Reading, when the 5th Battalion of the Royal Berkshire Regiment unexpectedly captured the Infantry Training Centre at Brock Barracks and Ranikhet Camp: 'Never before did an exultant enemy receive so warm a welcome.'

The camp was vastly improved for the arrival of the 327th Glider Infantry in 1943, part of the United States 101st Airborne (Screaming Eagles) Division, who were billeted at the camp, and many enduring friendships were made during their eighteen month stay.

Another part of the Division was billeted at Basildon Park, where they also trained before leaving for the D-Day landings of 1944. When the Division left, one section of the camp was being used for prisoners of war while the rest was taken over by people who found themselves without any other housing. Although this section was divided from the prisoners by only a single road, it was described as a very happy community, something like a holiday camp, with communal washing; the huts, warm in winter, were often divided for two families depending on how many children there were. The Council took it over before rehousing all the families.

From 1954 Ranikhet Camp was used by the Royal Army Pay Corps. Houses were built for use as married quarters, which were subsequently incorporated into Warnford Road. By 1960 the camp had been dismantled and a housing estate built on the land.

OTHER ACTIVITIES

The Home Guard had several ARP posts in Tilehurst. B8 still stands outside St Michael's Church, and another can be seen in Blagrave Recreation Ground. One Sunday morning in 1942 the Home Guard held an exercise which was known as 'The Battle of Tilehurst'; sadly it was reported that there was lack of cooperation or interest by the civilian population.

There was still a pillbox at Beansheaf Farm as late as 1979, although it is no longer there, and a big concrete air-raid shelter remains under the grass at The Triangle. During the war, children thought it was 'great fun' when they had to gather inside for air raids.

Other war-time memories include going to the Village Hall every other Wednesday evening and paying 6*d* to dance to music played on a wind-up gramophone; on Saturday evenings there was a live band. A trip to the Rex cinema at the bottom of Norcot Hill was a highlight. The highest price for a seat was 1*s* 6*d*, but those watching either had to leave early as the last bus was at 9 p.m. or face the walk up Norcot Hill in the dark because of the black-out.

The Civil Defence parade past the War Memorial, 1942.

Tilehurst was fortunate in escaping any direct bombing, but one incident did occur when a Canadian, flying a Blenheim trainer aircraft, hit 'the buckets' and came down near Broomfield Road. Two bombs were off-loaded by a German bomber returning from a raid in the Midlands, falling on land opposite what is now St Birinus Church. There were also reports of a bomb coming down in fields in the Langley Hill area, possibly the same one that was reported as falling on Blagrave Hospital causing slight damage to the boiler house and to a dairy nearby.

Grafton Road with the 'prefabs' after the Second World War. (L77/5. The Rural History Centre, University of Reading)

CHAPTER TEN

People of Note

THE PINCENTS

The family seat of the Pincents family, also recorded as Pinsens or Pinzums, was in Sulhampstead in the thirteenth century. In 1316 Gilbert Pincents' son, Edmund, exchanged the family land in Sulhampstead for some land in Tilehurst owned by Reading Abbey. Edmund remained in the parish until 1342 when the family name disappears. In 1494–5 a Margaret Sambourne, a widow, acquired the land. It descended through her family until it was sold with Southcote Manor to an Anthony Blagrave in 1598. The land remained in the Blagrave family and in 1708 passed to another Anthony Blagrave, and then to his son, John Blagrave, when he purchased the Manor of Tilehurst about 1759.

THE KENTWOODS

A Manor of Kentwood was held by Reading Abbey and later by Sir Peter Vanlore, under Tilehurst Manor. In the fourteenth century a family settled in the north of Tilehurst and took its name from the area, Nicholas Kentwood being recorded as a parishioner in 1341. There is mention of a Sir John Kentwood, whose cousin and

Pincents Farm, *c.* 1920.

heir was William Fettiplace, who later held the manor in the early sixteenth century. When that family line ceased, the Manor of Kentwood moved to the Dunch family. Interestingly, Edmund Dunch, who died in 1719, was a cousin of Oliver Cromwell.

SIR FRANCIS ENGLEFIELD

The manor of Tilehurst was held by Reading Abbey until the dissolution of the monasteries in the 1530s. In 1545 it was granted to Sir Francis Englefield, High Sheriff of Berkshire and Oxfordshire, who became a chief officer in the household of Princess Mary. He was a Catholic, and was imprisoned in the Tower of London after disobeying an order that Mass should no longer be said in the house of the princess. He was freed when Mary came to the throne in 1553, and he sat in the House of Commons as Knight of the Shire for the County of Berkshire.

In 1555 Sir Francis was a member of a commission looking into the practice of witchcraft. Later he took part in an enquiry into a conspiracy against the queen. When Queen Elizabeth I came to the throne in 1558 Sir Francis left for Spain, and his lands became forfeit in 1585 when Tilehurst passed back to the crown. Sir Francis ended his days in exile; he became blind and died in 1596. He was buried at Valladolid in Spain.

THE BLAGRAVES

The Blagrave family held a lot of land and property in both Tilehurst and Reading. Many distinguished members of this family have lived in and around the town. It is extremely difficult to determine which part of the family is which as many had the same Christian name.

In the thirteenth century a member of the family had a licence to fortify a moat, which was fed by Holy Brook. Some sources, however, suggest that the moated Southcote Manor was built in the late sixteenth century for Sir Anthony Blagrave by his brother, Sir John Blagrave, who became a famous mathematician, one of the first to study mathematics as a pure and exact science, and the author of *The Mathematical Jewel*. Sir John had been given land in Southcote by his father in 1591. Sir John latterly lived in Southcote Lodge where he died in 1611. The manor would probably have been involved in the siege of Reading in 1643.

There is also a George Blagrave of Kentwood, one of a large family, who was buried in Purley Church in 1709.

There is a story about a Jonathan Blagrave who, in 1723, had sold corn in Reading and, having had more than enough to drink to celebrate his success, was boasting about the money he had made. He was attacked on his way home, sustained a fractured skull and died near The Roebuck.

When John Blagrave purchased the Manor of Tilehurst from Benjamin Child in the 1750s, he pulled down the original Calcot House, built in the 1620s by Peter Vanlore, and rebuilt it. He was possibly the biggest landowner and the most influential member of the family in Tilehurst. Eliza Blagrave, his daughter, married Martin Routh in 1820.

In 1847 Colonel John Henry Blagrave, of the Berkshire Militia, was Lord of the

Southcote Manor with the detached watch tower; both were demolished in 1921. (D/L 4/110. The Rural History Centre, University of Reading)

Manor and lived at Calcot Park. The park was described as 'a handsome park well stocked with deer'. After the death of John Henry Blagrave, the estate was sold by Barry Blagrave, his eldest son, in 1918. The estate comprised some sixty-one lots which included ten farms, Southcote Manor (which by this time had 'an incomplete wooden bridge over a moat'), Southcote Lodge and Calcot Place, Pincents Farm ('probably one of the most ancient in Berkshire and the site of a Roman Villa'), two Ford's Farms (the one on the south side of the Bath Road gives its name to the present estate) and five thickly stocked woods.

The Blagrave family held Calcot Park until 1929 when an eighteen hole golf-course was created, the mansion being used as the clubhouse. This was subsequently changed into flats when a purpose-built clubhouse was put up. Behind the old mansion is a lake fed by a spring.

The Blagraves were always good landowners, taking an interest in all the people connected with their estates. They donated the land for the recreation ground which opened in 1894 and bears their name. They sold part of their land and gave a financial donation towards a hospital. They started a small school in Calcot and were influential in the National School. Herbert Blagrave died in 1981, a millionaire and one of the last surviving members of the Blagrave family.

SIR PETER VANLORE

After the death of Sir Francis Englefield in 1596, the Manor of Tilehurst passed from the crown and was leased and sold to people of wealth. In 1604 it came into the possession of Peter Vanlore.

Peter Vanlore was born in Holland in 1547. He became a banker and money lender in Utrecht, and eventually came to England as a Protestant refugee, probably in connection with the cloth trade. He was naturalized in 1607 and knighted by James I in November 1621.

He built himself a house in Calcot Park on the site of the present Calcot House, and married Jacoba Thibault, the daughter of a wealthy London merchant. They had one son and ten daughters. He became known as 'Old Sir Peter' to distinguish him from his son, also Peter. Old Sir Peter died in 1627 aged eighty. After his death one of his grand-daughters, also named Jacoba, and her husband, Henry Zinzan, lived in the house at Calcot. It was subsequently demolished. In 1638 Sir Edward Powell, Bt., son-in-law of Sir Peter, built the south aisle of St Michael's Church in order to erect a monument to Sir Peter and his wife, showing them recumbent on an altar tomb with their children grouped below them. Although the monument has been slightly damaged and altered over the years, it remains a remarkable memorial. An old water-colour hangs inside the church, which shows how the memorial looked originally.

WILLIAM LLOYD

William Lloyd was born in 1627, the son of a Tilehurst vicar. He was educated at home and went on to Oxford University. He became Bishop of St Asaph, during which time King James II issued the second Declaration of Indulgence with directions for it to be read in every church and chapel throughout the country. He became one of the seven bishops sent to the Tower of London in 1688 for opposing this. Lloyd was the leader of this group and caused quite a stir when he was brought before the court at Westminster. Enthusiastic supporters mobbed and tried to kiss him or his clothing. The bishops were found not guilty. He went on to become Bishop of Lichfield and Coventry, and then Worcester.

In 1712 Lloyd had an audience with Queen Anne. By this time he was convinced that he could interpret the prophecies in the scriptures and he told the queen that there would be a war of religion in four years time, that France would side with England as Protestant and popedom would be destroyed. He spoke as an anti-Papist, but probably was mentally unsound at the time. He lived to be ninety-one.

FRANCES KENDRICK

> Bachelors of every station
> Mark this strange but true relation
> Which to you in brief I bring
> Never was a stranger thing.
>
> from *The Berkshire Lady*

In the early 1700s Frances Kendrick was a very beautiful and very independent-minded seventeen year old. As her mother had also died Frances had inherited Calcot Park from her late father, Sir William Kendrick of Whitley Park.

Benjamin Child was a young attorney who lived in London. He was staying at the home of his uncle, a brewer, near Abingdon, when they were all invited to attend a family wedding of the Pleydells in Reading in 1707. Benjamin had the vague idea of picking up a country heiress as a wife as he was a handsome young man but had debts from his extravagant living in London.

The wedding consisted of three or four days of balls, banquets and routs, and it was during the festivities that Frances and Benjamin met. Frances had danced with Benjamin and at once determined to marry him, but he thought she had another alliance and so danced with other young ladies, hoping to find one he could marry. Frances thought that her obvious wealth might cause a barrier between them and so she wrote an anonymous letter to him, as if from a man, indicating that 'he' (Frances) had been slighted and challenging him to a duel. Benjamin, being quite uncertain as to why he was being challenged, and by which 'man', arrived at a place which is described variously as:

> at the entrance to Calcot Park, at the foot of the slope where there is a fountain, an hour after sunrise, and defend your insolence as best you may with a sword . . .

or

> a small open space of ground, surrounded by trees and bushes, near Tilehurst Church, at 6 o'clock next morning.

Here he waited and was soon confronted by a masked lady who insisted that he should fight her or, if he did not, then he must marry her. Once Benjamin discovered that his opponent was a lady, he decided he might just as well marry her. Frances had already made all the wedding arrangements, and the ceremony took place in St Mary's Church in The Butts, Reading, later that day, the bride refusing to remove her mask until after the wedding. The couple returned to Calcot House where Frances finally revealed her identity and when Benjamin happily accepted her beauty and her fortune. They had three daughters, one of whom died as a child, and tragically Frances herself died when she was only thirty-five.

Benjamin remained at Calcot until 1759, when he sold all his property to Sir John Blagrave of Southcote, with the exception of the area now known as Prospect Park. Benjamin then decided he wanted to remain in the house even though he had sold it, and it is said that the roof had to be removed to make him leave. He still had a small house called Diles, said to be on the site of a farm on the edge of what is now Prospect Park, which he had inherited through the Kendrick side of the family, and he lived there until he died. He was said to have become an eccentric.

Both Frances and Benjamin Child are buried in St Mary's Church. Prospect Park was left to their elder daughter. It was sold around 1813 to John Englebert Liebenrood.

The story of this couple is told in ballad form in *The Berkshire Lady*, although it has probably been somewhat embroidered in the telling.

DR MARTIN JOSEPH ROUTH

Here is a figure larger than life. Martin Joseph Routh was born in 1755, in Suffolk, the eldest of thirteen children. His mother was a descendant of Archbishop Laud (a

Dr Martin Joseph Routh.

Reading man). In 1791 Routh became a very young President of Magdalen College, Oxford, and two months later a Doctor of Divinity. He was presented to the living of St Michael's Church, Tilehurst, by Dr Sheppard, his brother-in-law and a wealthy benefactor, and became Rector from 1810 to 1854. However, he only came to his 'country living' during vacations, when he arrived in his carriage and pair and always wearing a wig, which was just one of his eccentricities. In *Dr Routh*, R.D. Middleton says that:

> of the importance in the history of the Church of England of Martin Joseph Routh there can be no question, and it is hardly an exaggeration to describe him as one of the most interesting and remarkable figures who have ever appeared in Oxford.

Dr Routh also exercised considerable influence in the setting up of the Episcopal Church in America.

In 1820, at the age of sixty-five, he married Eliza Agnes Blagrave, the daughter of John Blagrave of Calcot Park, who was only thirty. He used to walk to Theale and back, where his sister, Mrs Sheppard, had built a church. He lived to be ninety-nine years old, and Routh Lane is named after him.

Dr Routh was succeeded as Rector by his nephew, Revd John Routh, who was born in 1817. His wife became a Roman Catholic and to avoid embarrassment he had a private road made, which avoided the village, and took her carriage and pair. The road became known as Lovers Lane and led to Grovelands. It was later the subject of the extraordinary court case described in Chapter Two. John Routh died in 1905. He had ten children.

JOHN ENGLEBERT LIEBENROOD

The Liebenrood family owned a considerable amount of land in Tilehurst. Around 1800 John Englebert Liebenrood bought the estate now known as Prospect Park, and lived at Diles as the house was then known. In 1854 Captain John Liebenrood was living at Prospect House. The estate was sold by Major Englebert Liebenrood to a speculator, Thomas Fidler, who sold it on to Reading Corporation in 1902 to be used as a public park. Liebenrood also gave the land for the Village Hall.

Although both Captain Liebenrood and his wife, Lucy, are buried in Purley Church, there is an epitaph to Lucy in St Michael's Church. The epitaph reads:

> although elevated in marriage to a rank of life far beyond her pretensions and expectations, by undeviating good and virtuous conduct gained the love and esteem of all who knew her. The poor never wanted a friend and advocate while she lived, she was the friend of all. This, despite having to suffer a severity that few mortals have experienced, which she bore with pious resignation until death relieved her in 1829.

MORTIMER MENPES

Born in 1859 in Port Adelaide, South Australia, Mortimer Menpes was a painter and etcher. His education took place mostly in Australia, but he came to England for further art training and exhibited several of his works at the Royal Academy. He married when he was twenty and had four children.

In 1900 he became a war artist in South Africa. He later wrote several books on famous people, some of which he illustrated. He made very good reproductions of several of the Old Masters. He was joint founder of the Menpes Press in London and was said to be a well-known London figure, moving in 'high circles'.

None of this explains why Menpes set up a large fruit farm in Long Lane, known as Menpes Fruit Farm Limited, which included the Carnation Nurseries at Purley, established in 1907.

Menpes died in 1938. His daughter lived in a thatched cottage in Westwood Row which burnt down.

CECIL ALDIN

Born in Slough, Cecil Aldin lived at Sulhamstead Abbots. He was a nineteenth-century artist, who travelled around the countryside and painted a series of pictures of old pubs and coaching houses.

Aldin was particularly interested in painting hunting scenes, and from 1915 to 1919 was Master of the South Berkshire Hunt. The hounds were kennelled at World's End, near the corner with Burghfield Road where Old Kennels Court now stands. In 1910 the area became busier so the kennels moved to Purley and eventually in 1955 out to Mortimer. He also provided kennels for a friend's Basset hounds, which he hunted two afternoons a week for the season. While he was Master, he had an ex-army hut converted at the kennels to use as his studio and to house his own dogs during the day.

The South Berkshire Hunt at The Roebuck in the 1940s.

At the start of the First World War Aldin organized the provision of horses for the army. Thousands of suitable horses were needed and had to be supplied with tack.

He illustrated many books, among them some editions of Kipling's *Jungle Stories* and Dickens' *Pickwick Papers*. He also illustrated his own autobiography.

ARTHUR NEWBERY

Arthur Newbery was born in 1864. From 1914 to 1921 he was a member of Reading Borough Council. He owned a considerable amount of land between Armour and Kentwood Hills, which he gave for development. He also gave a building on Armour Hill for use as a public library, which he opened in 1931. Although it ceased to be the library in 1960, the building still stands as Newbery Lodge.

Newbery was a Methodist and gave the land on which the Kentwood Methodist Church is built, and he owned the house which is now called The Link in School Road.

He lived in Daneshill on Elsley Road, and in 1932 gave the park which bears his name to the town. He also owned other land in Tilehurst.

In 1940 Newbery opened a very high class shop selling new and antique furniture, as well as soft furnishings. The shop was situated on the corner of Queen Victoria Street and Friar Street in Reading. In 1945 he left Tilehurst to live in Bristol, later moving to Lyme Regis. He sold his furniture shop in 1949 and died in 1961.

SIR FELIX POLE

Born in 1877, Pole obtained a job with the GWR in Swindon at the age of fourteen, and by 1921, at the age of forty-four, he was the youngest known General Manager.

The view from what is now Arthur Newbery Park, looking north over Kentwood Hill to the potteries and water tower, *c.* 1930.

In 1921 he set up 'land cruises', which included staying in railway hotels. He was knighted in 1924.

Sir Felix had his own private train with a viewing window at the back. There is a tale that all workmen had to stand aside to let this train go past and that, on one such occasion, Sir Felix saw a lengthman smoking. (The old 'Rule Book' given to every member of staff stated that smoking and eating were prohibited when 'on duty'.) He is said to have stopped the train and sacked the man on the spot.

Sir Felix lived at Calcot Place and kept the Kennet Valley Nurseries along Burghfield Road. He used Tilehurst station and travelled from there to his home in his carriage, and later in his car.

He left the railways in 1929 and took up the chairmanship of the Associated Electrical Industries Limited. Although he lost his sight he continued to work for many years.

He was the first President of Tilehurst Eisteddfod, and enjoyed spending some of his leisure time fishing in the Kennet.

Sir Felix died in 1956 and train drivers are said to have sounded their whistle as they went along the Reading to Newbury line as they remembered him.

WILLIAM MCILROY

William Ewart Clarke McIlroy was born in 1893. He fought in the First World War and was wounded at the Somme and sent home in 1916. He became Managing Director of Messrs William McIlroy Ltd in 1923 (his father was also William McIlroy). This was the department store in Oxford Road which ran from Cheapside to West Street. It was one of the architectural wonders of the town at the time, and had huge windows on both ground floor and first floor levels. It was sometimes known as 'Reading's Crystal Palace' or 'Macs'.

The store was said to have a café on the top floor from which could be seen a plot of land that could have been part of Minchins Farm, although it is likely to have been a piece of land left over after building had been completed all around. The land was bought by William McIlroy so that the open space could remain on view from his premises, and it was made into a park which bears his name. Although the park remains, the shop ceased trading in 1955. The building still stands opposite the Broad Street Mall. Looking at the upper part of the building it is still possible to imagine it as the impressive store that it once was.

McIlroy was made a JP in 1934, was Mayor of Reading from 1938 to 1943 and was made a Freeman of Reading in 1943. He lived at Carrick-a-Rede, Clevedon Road, Tilehurst-on-Thames and died in 1963.

THOMAS AITKEN

Thomas Aitken lived in Tilehurst and in 1922 was a foreman employed by the Tilehurst, Pangbourne and District Water Company. Once, in the course of his duties he arrived with an engineer to inspect a set of water pumps at the pumping station in Gipsy Lane.

The two men descended halfway down a well shaft that was 120 ft deep and which contained some 80 ft of water. The engineer was making his way across a staging plank just below the pumps when it broke, causing him to plunge deeper into the well shaft. Fortunately, however, he was caught on an old piece of staging lower down, and he managed to grasp a piece of iron bar attached to it. As he fell the lamp fell with him and the well shaft was plunged into darkness.

Mr Thomas Aitken.

Aitken had just managed to save himself from falling by holding on to the iron ladder which led to the top of the shaft. He could hear his colleague crying out for help from below so, feeling his way, he worked round to an old, disused ladder which was extremely slippery and had several rungs missing. He made his way down, but the ladder did not reach as far as the old staging. Aitken did not give up, however, and using any foothold he could, he eventually reached the point where his colleague lay, his strength nearly given out.

Aitken managed to lift him onto a safer ledge a little way above and then set off back up the shaft to get ropes with which he then secured the engineer and brought him to the top. Shaken and bruised the engineer had suffered a dislocated shoulder and a badly damaged foot which later had to be amputated. However, he had been saved from falling to his certain death by Aitken.

For his courage Thomas Aitken was presented with the Edward Medal, sometimes known as the Victoria Cross of Industry, by the king.